M000014281

This book is dedicated to those who want to improve but don't know how to go about it.

Ask questions and listen my friends.

Outline

1. Introduction

This book's progenitor was multiple phone calls and conversations with friends who after a lot of beating around the bush would nervously ask me something like "I know you're good with money and I think I need some advice…" They would then explain their situation and in a panicked rush, ask me "what should I being doing?". "Should I get a car? How much should I spend on the car? How much should I be saving? What should I do with those savings?" While I relished being able to help them out of experience and knowledge, after a few friends reaching out, I realized that most of my friends had no clue how to manage their money, especially when they had very little of it.

I'm not going to pretend I have a particularly diverse set of friends from all economic backgrounds, but I will say this - financial issues and money management are not limited to certain socio-economic status, gender, ethnicity, or race. Some of my friends were born rich beyond belief and they were asking me if I saved for retirement and how they could. Some of my friends were making less than 30k a year and had amassed an impressive amount of money but were just sitting on it. Some just had no clue - they didn't see saving as something they needed to do, but wanted to know why I said no to something because "I couldn't afford it".

One pattern emerged: people my age (20s-30s) just don't talk about money - not with their friends, not with their parents, and sometimes not with their significant others. Well, they'll talk about money in terms of how much student debt they have or how poor they are, but it's not cool to talk about retirement or saving for a house. It wasn't always about not having a good example - you can't learn if there's no discussion or explanation of why.

As much as I wish my parents had handed me a Financial Bible when I was 18 and we had a lengthy discussion, it didn't work that way for me either. Actually, growing up I vehemently disagreed with most of my parents' financial decisions and how they affected me (spoiler: they were right). But, my dad did hand me a Vanguard account when I was 18 that had a few thousand dollars in it from all the times someone gave me cash for Christmas or a birthday and it "disappeared" with dad. Huh. Maybe that's better than a Money Bible.

A lot of the advice in here comes from them (thanks Mom and Dad!) but a lot of it was also honed by my life experiences, friends' life experiences, my research, and trial and error. I do feel like I have been extremely successful and made a lot out of what I was given and turned it into more (reinvestment!), which is why friends came to me in the first place with their questions. They had heard me say things like I was saving ⅓ of my graduate stipend and wanted to know what magic lied behind it and why was I trying so hard to do such a thing.

From my few conversations with friends, I wrote a few blog posts that received more attention than I expected - people were curious. Once again, there was this pattern of people looking for open, non-judgemental discussion (re: reading my blog post but me having no insight on their finances). However, my older friends had lots of advice and pearls of wisdom to share. Yes, they probably weren't writing a Financial Bible for their children, but they were more than happy to tell me how I was being dumb for not buying a house when I could (spoiler: they were right) and that I should be saving more for retirement (spoiler: they're probably right).

As I wrote, saved, and lived more, I realized that it was important that I write down what I have learned in the past 10 years and share it with whoever is looking for non-judgemental help on money and doesn't know where to look or who can they trust (valid). If there is only one thing that you take from this book, it's that it is never too late to start putting feet in the right direction. Obviously, the sooner you do it, the better! However, starting tomorrow is better than never starting.

That's what this is all meant to be - encouragement and steps you can take to improve your situation. I distill it down to seven topics and start with the most important and descend in importance from there. To be honest, even as I wrote this I had to re-evaluate my current life choices and ask if I was being a hypocrite. More than I would like to admit, I had to answer that yes. So, I adjusted the way I was living, again. It felt great to go back and remember to say no and make trade-offs, like I was re-connecting with the stronger version of myself who was focused on achieving her dreams. Even for the experts, it's good to go back and refresh.

The following chapters may be things you're already doing or they may be things you've never thought of before. They may be things that you're completely incapable of doing. The goal is to re-evaluate your own methods and try to improve them; if you read this book and find yourself doing that, then your time and energy have been well spent in reading this. If not, then maybe you should write a book because you might have more advice than I do.

2. Learn to Say No

Isn't this one obvious? We hear this all the time - "Honey, you have to learn to say no... you can't do violin and volleyball and get a 4.0, you'll explode" or "You have to say no to her otherwise she'll just keep using you!". However, learning to say no to others is generally taught and advised in the context of time or personal energy resources and not in terms of money. Hence, why saying no isn't obvious.

People who say no in the context of money... we're taught those are stingy, heartless people. They don't give to charity. They don't help the poor. They'd push a 3- year-old out of the way to pick up a nickel off the street. They talk about burdens on the tax system and count their pennies every night. The person you probably just conjured up in your mind is not someone who you want to be at all. You want to be generous and kind, and you'd rather be shit poor than the Ebenezer Scrooge described above.

The thing is, you can say no and not be Ebneezer Scrooge. You just need to reframe how you're saying no.

Try looking at it like this: you want to go out with your friends - it's Sarah's birthday and she wants to go to her favorite Cuban restaurant. You like Sarah - she's OK, and your best friends Michelle and Clare (because you, of course, have two best friends) are going, so duh, you're going to go. You go to the Cuban restaurant, everyone is ordering dinner, so even though you're not really hungry, you feel obligated to order a meal. Oh, and everyone is ordering drinks, so you order a beer too. You all skip on dessert because you are financially responsible women and you go to pay your bill (and add in Sarah's, you all decided to chip in to buy her dinner). Your bill comes to $32.

But the evening isn't over - Sarah wants to go to a bar after. It is her 24th birthday and she's single and cute - you can't blame her. Naturally, she doesn't want to go alone. You're kind of tired and now full from Cuban food and want to go home to snuggle your dog, but Michelle and Clare (besties!) are going, so ... you go too. You order a beer and then a mixed drink later on in the night. $15, not too bad. You got the cheap beer and the special mixed drink. You take an uber home (responsible!) and that's another $13, so for the total of the night... you're at $60. Yikes.

To some of you reading, that's a cheap night and to some of you, that's a devastating budget breaking night. It doesn't matter - what does matter is that it's $60 gone and was that a memorable night or did you just feel like you were going because other people wanted you to go? It's pretty common knowledge that science has shown people are happier spending their money on experiences rather than things [1] but if those experiences are bleh, are you really happier?

But maybe $60 doesn't matter, it's just one night. I know I wasn't even that popular of a person in college and I was invited to dinners and parties like this all the time - probably at least 20 a year. 20 x $60 = $1200 a year on dinner parties and bar nights for people that you may not even like.

How many memorable birthday dinners have you gone to? What if I told you that you could watch the sunrise at the Grand Canyon with your besties Clare and Michelle (drive all night, karaoke the whole way!) or you could go to 12 birthday dinners? I mean, you can pick the latter, but we'll talk about that later in Chapter 3.

So that's why you have to learn to say no or reframe potentially expensive situations into less expensive and/or more meaningful experiences. I promise, you won't become Mr. Scrooge either.

If you don't say no, and I know many people in this bucket, you end up overspending. Guaranteed. I don't know a single "always yes (money doesn't matter)" person who isn't in debt or barely living paycheck to paycheck (or in some cases, trust fund check to trust fund check). We all have to say no, and I'm encouraging you to say it more often and on your own terms.

Diving in, there are many ways to say no and many people (including yourself) you're going to have to say no to… and you won't always be successful. I slip off the wagon often saying no to people, but then I look at my credit card statement, yell at myself a bit, and realize I need to be disciplined again. Not because I need a certain amount of no in my life, but more that I am a disappointed in myself for caving to societal pressure instead of focusing on what I want out of life.

Saying no to yourself

Let's start with the easy one, say no to yourself. This is basic self-control, and assuming you passed Kindergarten, you have the fundamentals down (wait in line for the bathroom instead of peeing pants, check).

When/how do you say no? Let's start with big things. You have 2 weeks of vacation and you want to do something epic that involves beaches and kayak rentals. After discussing with some friends and internet searching, you find 3 options:

(1) Going to Lake Michigan in July near your friend (who is super hot to make this more tempting) Karen (or Tom, if you like men) and staying at their summer house in Traverse City, Michigan. $.

(2) Going to Aruba with a tour group and staying at a really nice hotel. $$$.

(3) Going to the Florida Keys and doing a self-guided tour hopping island to island with two friends (they aren't as hot as Tom/Karen but you get the idea). $$.

Those all sound great, really. A vacation is a vacation. Some of you aren't as enchanted with (1) because it's not exotic enough, that's fine. But if you're picking between (2) and (3) then, why pick Aruba if you're going to derive the same amount of fun and excitement hopping keys? It just costs you more money (unless it's a life dream to go to Aruba and stay in fancy hotels, then you pick 2!). So you pick 3, and you save yourself about $800.

Look at that, you said no. To yourself. And you lost almost nothing. What if half your friends are going to Aruba and a few are going to the Keys and you still choose the Keys? You'll still probably have a solid vacation with lots of experiences and bond with people but you'll still be $800 richer. That's huge.

That one may be obvious, but let's look at some of the insidious ways people get caught not saying no. You go to order a latte, you feel a little more tired than usual, so you order a large. $4.80. What's the difference between a small and large latte? $1.20. Hmmm. Doesn't look like much, but once again... 50 lattes in a year mean $60. Doesn't sound like that much either, but was that little bit of extra latte for a year worth a night out with what's her name (Sarah! That's it!)?

Just saying no in a small way occasionally adds up, even if it's getting a shirt you wanted in your second favorite color because it's on sale, etc. If you always say 'yes' to yourself to optimize happiness, then nothing ever really feels like a treat or reward either. In Parks and Rec, they had a "Treat yo'self" day where you just splurged on everything you ever wanted for ONE day, and it was a glorious day.

My friend Liz is a master of the self-no to small things. I watched her throughout high school and college constantly say no unless something was deeply on sale or a need. Personally, I thought it was to a ridiculous extent at times, like saying no to a shirt she clearly loved, was on sale and cheap, and made her look like a 10 (well, she was always a 10 so maybe that's why). But she'd do it, over and over and over again, and guess what? Liz had very few expenses and never needed to work much to cover them; she got to spend a lot of time on the beach with her family and friends because she would say no to clothes and dinners, and that's priceless.

You may not be good at the no to small things - I mean, they are small things that inevitably generate momentary joy. Just try it - next time order the smaller latte or a plain coffee with milk. See if it still tastes good and save the medium latte for a celebration. Try ordering an appetizer instead of a full meal if you're not that hungry. Remember, the less you consume, the more environmentally friendly you are too (hey! Look at that Mr. Scrooge - you're now an environmental justice warrior!). There's a lot of good that can come from self-no'ing, just don't take it to the extreme and *become unhappy* because of your acerbicism (i.e. Anorexia, becoming a militant vegan who throws paint on people with fur coats, living naked on the streets, etc.).

Let's look at how these small no's can add up. This list is not comprehensive - see the Appendix at the end of "Small No Tips" for little ways to change what you do. We're going to look at 2 days of different budgeting to get a sense for how it adds up.

Date, Time, Event	"Save for when it matters" Steve	"Why be anything but Happy" Bob
10/1, 7 AM, Coffee Shop	Small coffee and donut special, .99 each, **$1.98**	Medium latte and cheese Danish, 4.00 + 2.79 = **$6.79**
10/1, 10 AM, Online Shopping for Winter Jacket	Last season model but matches needed specs, **$62.50**	Latest tech, in bright color **$199**
10/1, 12 PM, Lunch!	Brought bag lunch, homemade burrito! **$1.50** in ingredients	Cafeteria, **$6.50**
10/1, 3 PM, Snack	Granola bar from home bought in bulk, **$1**	Vending machine, **$1.75**
10/1, 6 PM, Happy Hour!	1 beer, then home for dinner (includes ingredients for	Margarita and burrito for dinner, **$16.75**

	dinner) **$6**	
10/2, 8 AM, Groceries!	Buy stuff on sale to make meals for the week, buy discounted brands when possible **$70**	Important to get organic and exactly what I want (double stuff Oreos, Ben & Jerry's ice cream) **$110**
10/2, Daytime, Activity!	Ride Bicycle around the park with friends, get ice cream after **$3**	Play paintball and get ice cream afterward **$45**
10/2, Night time, see Play	Get discounted tickets, OK seats **$50**	Get the good seats! **$100**
Totals	**$245.98**	**$485.79**

Did this surprise you how different these numbers are? Bob outspent Steve by almost 100%, which is crazy. That means that Bob would have to make more than 100% of Steve's salary (because of taxes!) in order to have the same savings as Steve after a year of this. Even if we pull out the big purchase of that winter coat, we're still looking at a difference of **$245.98 to $183.48,** or Steve spending 75% of what Bob is spending. That adds up in a big way when you start thinking in terms of a yearly budget; Bob spending $10,000 would be the same as Steve spending $7,500, which means Steve can go kayaking in the Keys without worry of going into debt.

You don't have to be as aggressive as Steve above, but it is healthy to ask yourself "do I need this?" and see if there is a less expensive and nearly as good option. Save the splurges for treats and celebrations and you'll appreciate them more.

Saying no to others

Oof this is hard - I won't lie. We all cave to peer pressure more often than any of us would like to admit. But you **absolutely** have to say no to others at some point in order to live an even remotely happy life. We are taught adages from a young age like "Give a man a fish, you feed him for a day. Teach a man to fish, and he's fed for life" that reflect reframing saying no to others for their own benefit (and our own too).

I'm not encouraging you to become a no-master, who just says no to everything and anything regardless of fun or cost factor (fun costs money! bad!). No... I'm asking you to think critically about if the happiness gained balances with the cost of the activity or if you're just doing said activity because other people are.

There are two types of money asks from others: silent asks and direct asks. A silent ask is when all your friends have it, so shouldn't you have it too? The answer is equally non-verbalized - you either get it or you don't. A direct ask is when your friends ask you to do something with them and you have to respond yes or no.

I struggle with the silent asks and often have to check myself. A personal example is that I'm an avid/borderline obsessive cyclist in my free time. I love bikes, and they are a ridiculously expensive hobby that brings me irreplaceable joy, and nothing feels better than new bike day (which is exactly what it sounds like). Most of my equally obsessive bike friends have justified their hobby by saying "I use this instead of a car, so I can buy a $10,000 bicycle". OK, true, bicycles are way cheaper than cars. But being around this school of thought started to change the way I saw spending money on bicycles and normalized this outlandish spending. Suddenly a $4000 bicycle seemed "more than reasonable", and I was suckered in. New bike day felt awesome.

However, my boyfriend and I soon after acquired another bicycle from a summer intern which we wanted for commuting. Even though that bike cost $200 (re: I could have bought 20 of them for the cost of my super nice bike), new bike day felt just as awesome and we were almost just as fast on the second bike. Why in the world did we spend so much money on our super nice bicycles?

Answer: the silent asks. Damn it, they got us. None of our friends actually cared if we got a nice bicycle, but we wanted to be accepted and admired in the way we admired them when they got a fancy-pants bicycle. We cared, and so we spent a lot of money (re: time) to be part of the cool bike club.

How do you resist the silent asks? You ask yourself if you need it, emphasis on **need.** Do you need a nice car? Do you need designer clothes? Do you need an electric toothbrush? Sometimes you do! Sometimes you're in a line of work that requires you to have status symbols in order to be successful (i.e. you can't show up as a realtor on a $200 bicycle to show a house, except maybe in Portland). If you don't **need** it, then you're going to read Chapter 3 and ask yourself if you want it badly enough to justify how much time and energy it will cost you.

And the direct asks? Others struggle with the direct asks more, especially if you are someone trying to be included in a new community or attain popularity. You feel (silently) that you need to accept in order to make friends, and, I won't lie, you sometimes need to in order to show reciprocal interest in friendship. It's a Catch 22 to be sure, but there are ways to mitigate.

First, repeat after me, it's OK to say no to people if you don't want to do something. If you don't like Football, don't agree to go to a Football game just because the cute guy asks you to go (sigh, this just became a dating advice paragraph too). Yes, if you just say "no" he may get the wrong idea that you hate him. Instead, propose something else that you both may enjoy doing and is more within your budget. You: "Hey, to be honest, I'm not a huge Football fan, but I love roller skating - want to go to the park and skate on Saturday?" Him: "Wow, I love how honest and truthful you are, my ex didn't tell me she hated Football until after 6 months of dating and skating sounds great".

See? All good things from saying no, except you never actually said no! Wow! You redirected and changed the activity from an expensive one to a less expensive and more enjoyable one.

Let's revisit Sarah's dinner... what could you have done there? One, you could have left after dinner or showed up for drinks after - that would have cut your costs by half. Two, you could have said outright no and done something else that night, like write a book or go out with other friends that you liked more (but BFFs Michelle and Clare were at the dinner!). Three, you could have proposed an alternative solution if Sarah was a close friend. "Hey Sarah... I know you love this restaurant but wouldn't a SURPRISE party be more fun?" and then throw her a surprise party at your place and have everyone chip in. Hell, get her a pinata and fill it with mini bottles, she'll love you forever and it'll still be cheaper than everyone buying dinner.

If Sarah really wants to go to dinner at her favorite Cuban restaurant and you don't really care that much, then don't go. Or if you care about Sarah a lot, go, but then realize that means you're prioritizing Sarah's happiness above your own. No one is making you go and buy things, and life gets expensive when you start doing things you don't care about because you can't say no. Pick the things you love and spend your time and money there, period. But in order to save friends and not be Mr. Scrooge, try reframing occasionally and see if people are looking for an excuse to socialize by going to a bar when you could come up with a more fun and cheaper solution (mini bottle pinataaaa). Also, find friends who like doing the same things you do, then these types of problems happen less often.

Summary

The first step to making a lot of a little is to say no. Sometimes you have to say no to nice things, fun things, great people, and even a good time, but you don't have to say no all the time. Every time you can say no though, it accumulates and you can do more with less money. Sometimes it is as simple as choosing coffee over a latte or last year's model instead of what's new. Try not to get caught up in "getting what everyone else has" and focus on your needs and happiness and the needs and happiness of those you care about.

Try "reframing" situations by taking a friend's expensive plan and proposing an alternative just-as-fun (or more!) night that is cheaper. You can say no without actually ever having to say no, still have friends, and not be shit poor. Talk about having your cake and eating it too!

3. What You Have Is Enough

Confession time, one of the inspirations for this book was a boyfriend of mine (gasp!). When we first started dating, he had a very different perspective on financial matters than I had, with a very different outcome (re: not good). He agreed his methodology wasn't working and he needed to change (never too late to change!) but the biggest sticking point he had trouble letting go of was this one - I thought he made enough money to be happy and meet his needs. Instead, he believed a lot of his problems could be solved by making more money, even just 10% more, and in his case, this simply wasn't true.

So full disclaimer before I launch in: for many people, what you have isn't actually enough. I won't even sugarcoat it, it's not enough, you live in poverty and can't feed you/your family. Don't be insulted by my chapter heading; instead, *magic word* reframe it - what you have is what you have so you need to work with it because... there aren't any other choices. It needs to be enough (somehow) because the only other choice is to give up, which is far worse. Keep fighting, keeping trying, and eventually you can't keep getting losing cards.

For the rest of you, which is most of you reading this book, you make enough money to meet your needs, be happy, and even (gasp) save money. Say it out loud – "I have enough" - stop using this as an excuse not to save.

Let's start by first dispelling a myth - that making more money will solve your budget constraints and you'll be able to save more money. It's just not true.

In your life, you're going to have a few massive pay jumps that allow you to radically change your day to day. I've seen this happen to most of my friends throughout their 20s, and everyone will encounter a massive pay jump at least once.

The first one happens with your first job. You went from having $0/month income to, by golly, minimum wage (or somewhere close to it). You're rich!

The next one happens if you go to college or get some sort of degree that allows you to take an entry-level position in a professional position; you're now making in the tens of thousands (you're *rich-er*!). Up the pyramid, the next massive pay jump some but not all of you may hit is the experienced professional or lower management position (hello six figures!). One more notch up would be upper-level management, and past that would be running your own company and making it, lottery winning, being born rich and investing wisely, etc.

No one reading this book should **depend on** achieving a 10 million dollars a year salary. According to IRS 2016 returns, 424,442 people had over $1,000,000 a year income, which was .2% of all Americans [2] and only 16,087 hit that magical 10 million dollar a year salary (0.01%).

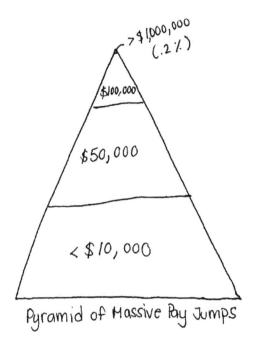

Pyramid of Massive Pay Jumps

Besides guiding you along to a "fuck rich people" attitude, the real goal of the Pyramid of Massive Pay Jumps is just to show you that you can't count on these to keep happening. With the massive pay increases, there are substantial quality in life changes (unless you say no to everything). Everything is a smaller fraction of your income, and so you can relax a bit and go to Sarah's meh dinner without feeling the consequence as much.

However, **do not use that** as an excuse to delay saving or paying off debt because the reality is, even when you hit that new pay grade, your life is going to adjust around it and it won't feel so massive. Even more, these massive pay jumps aren't sustainable. Once you stabilize in your career, you're looking at a 2-4% annual increase in your salary if you're lucky. You're probably going to be stuck there indefinitely until you hopefully retire because you've been saving.

The taxes also catch up to you. When I was in graduate school (level 2 on pyramid), I paid about 10% of my annual income in taxes; now (level 3), I pay a lot closer to 30%, which means to save 30%, my expenditures are down to 40% which is starting to look a lot like what my total annual income was before. Huh, I'm not actually that much richer - I live the same way I would have in graduate school if I had saved *nothing*.

There are some of you out there going, "exactly! You just need to keep living the way you did in graduate school/first job when you get new fancy paycheck and then you can pay off your debt and save for retirement". Can you even say that with a straight face? There are very few (and they are awesome no'ers, I assure you) that can pull off this because most of us, when handed a new paycheck, will go "cool, I want to buy a car now, and get a nicer place, etc.". So unless your no-fu is astounding after years of not no-ing yourself, let's come up with a real plan.

The silent asks will also compound. Your peers are going to have bigger paychecks too, and they are going to want to do things like get nice dinners and go on cool trips, not eat ramen noodles in your studio apartment where the plumbing doesn't work because you're still living like a student.

It's hard to break habits and create new ones. By always saving, you've built that habit and just naturally figure it into your budget. By aggressively saving, you think in terms of the future more and what you'll do with time/investments/being free! You want to be free and not have a boss? Save your money and don't spend it - it's that simple.

The common pushback I received in graduate school about my "aggressive saving" was that there was no point to it. Why save so much, >30% rather than 10% which would have covered emergencies, when it meant so little? Postgrad, I would make more in a few months than I did in a year of graduate work, and my savings could easily be matched shortly while working in industry. Oh, I have answers.

At some point in graduate school, I was meeting my savings goal of maxing out my Roth IRA every year and still having some extra, and the extra was starting to accumulate. Should it be a trip around the world? A new car? No... I can't tell you what possessed me, but I started calling this my house fund. The "little house fund that could" grew and grew and grew in the stock market and with steady additions. When I graduated, it had become something meaningful (the stock market did really well those years, it helped. Small gambles.).

I took this meaningful start, moved to Seattle, and worked for 1.5 years aggressively putting money away into house fund. When I found out my rent was going to go up by 30%, I said fuck you to the apartment I lived in and went house shopping. I found one and put a 30% down payment on it. The home buying process was simple and fairly straightforward for me - the houses that met my needs were well within budget.

But… here's the crazy part, the potential houses wouldn't have been affordable without that extra saving in graduate school. I would have needed to work another 6 months to hit the 20ish% down payment range, and by then the market would have increased. I would have had to move twice or bought a smaller place, and I would be paying rent for another 6 months, where 6 months x $2000 rent per month = $12000 down the drain. Wow, right? Not going to Sarah's birthday dinner parties that I never really wanted to go to anyway and saying no turned into a house, and has since saved me over $10,000 in just rent. That's a meaningful amount of money for anyone.

Where am I going with all of this? You have enough! More than enough! Or, er, it has to be enough! You can save, you can treat yourself occasionally, and you can prosper on what you have. You just may need to say no to a whole lot of things that you don't want to say no to in order to get there.

One of my former co-workers, a pretty successful software engineer, was complaining that he could barely afford to survive on his salary of 150k in the Seattle area. Yes, he had reasons why it was so impossibly hard for him to make due, but the reality was that he didn't appreciate what he had and what he could afford. Instead, he was overly focused on what adding another 50 k could do for his lifestyle, and he was miserable, feeling trapped in his own life. Yuck!! Don't be this person!! You won't be happy and guess what? That 50k pay bump isn't going to feel like enough.

In American culture, we're pushed constantly to spend to our max and live the lifestyle we can "afford". By "afford", America means "go into sustained but manageable debt indefinitely". In the past 20 years, we've normalized having a mortgage and enormous student debt. Even credit card debt is just "something that happens". It's not!! But no matter what pyramid bracket you're in, you'll be pushed to exceed the boundaries of your income, I guarantee it. Enough isn't enough until you decide it is.

Moral of this story is to accept the things you can not change right now and live within your means. I can't tell you exactly how much you should/can save on your budget - a lot of that comes down to personal choice (i.e. do you have children and want to pay for their college instead of taking them to Aruba every year?).

The thing I can tell you is that retiring is all about how little can you live off of relative to how much you make. The best way to retire early and spend all your days traveling? Save your money; saving 30% of your income towards retirement means that you're spending 70% and saving 30% so you'll need to work about 2 years to get 1 year of retirement. Saving 10%? You'll need to work for 9 years then at your current burn rate.

But let's not kid ourselves, you're in your 20s and retirement sounds impossibly far away. Right now you're trying to plan weddings, travel, and buying a home. Or maybe just trying not to be shit poor. You save because once you have a cash stockpile, you can start doing things like buying property and not paying rent (we'll talk about the math on that later). Saving money gives you choices - you can take a year off work and travel, you can deal with emergencies, you can splurge on a wedding and saving needs to happen now, not something for future you to deal with.

The question is how to save and determine enough is enough? There's a different way to do this for everyone, and some ways are better than others. My advice is to minimize expenses for 2-3 months - challenge yourself to see how little you can live off of. Be disciplined and smart. This sets your "baseline" for expenses - how much you can expect to spend every month.

Let's say your after-tax income is $3000 and your baseline (with rent, food, clothing, etc.) is $1700, so you have a surplus of $1300. Set aside a savings account that has at least 3 months expenses (so $5000-$6000 here, that's for car emergencies, etc.). After that is filled, I'd start putting away $1000 into an investment portfolio (to be discussed later in that chapter about how investing is easier than learning the alphabet). Make yourself do it - that's your real savings account, for a house, for retirement, or to travel the world. Notice how I only said $1000, not $1300; the extra $300 is your play money for saying no to Sarah's dinners and you can turn that into a European vacation, etc. We'll talk about that in the next chapter.

4. Everything is a Trade-Off

We like having definites - like being told "if you do A, you get B". Definites are comforting. It'd be great if someone told me every month that groceries would cost exactly $200, but the reality is sometimes I want to get brie instead of cheddar or I want to get eggnog when it's Christmas. Suddenly, my groceries don't cost $200 anymore, so where does that money get pulled from?

Well, the magic credit card won't tell you that you don't have another $5 for fancy cheese and eggnog, your rent is probably fairly fixed, and so maybe you have to pull it from your savings or your "get rid of college debt" fund. It's only $5, so not much harm...

But revisiting the latte paradigm in Chapter 1, we know these things, however small, do add up over time. So you find yourself asking - do I really want brie more than I want to go on a European vacation?

Wait? Who asks that, ever? Can you imagine some big burly dude in a red-and-black checkered shirt and black frame glasses holding up the fake French Brie at Kroger under fluorescent lighting and going "mmm if I get this now, it means I can't afford to go Europe next year and eat good Brie in France?"

But that's the reality - we make financial choices every day that control our goals, happiness, and lifestyle. The ability to say no is huge in stopping an exodus of money from your wallet, but the second part of not being shit poor is realizing once your budget has been set, everything you choose to buy means you don't get to buy something else. Shoes or wallet? New phone or new computer? New clothes or save for a bigger home?

A graduate school roommate and I took this principle to the extreme when we decided that we would heat our home in Ann Arbor, Michigan as little as possible in the winter and use the money we saved to buy clothes (which would then keep us warm instead, duh). I mean, it wasn't rocket science - it's very expensive to heat a home in Michigan in winter to comfortable levels. Yet, we saw this as wasted money - we'd rather wear an extra sweater in the house because that would mean we could buy a new sweater!

The beauty of this arrangement was that Xuejing and I were really happy with this decision. Yes, our guests shivered when we had them over for dinner (keep your coat on!) and the only time we felt warm was our 10 minute shower every day (bliss!). But... we saw it as a choice. We chose to feel cold/adversity because that now meant a reward that we wouldn't have been able to justify otherwise. New Clothes!

When I was young and my parents implemented this same policy, it wasn't nearly as satisfying though. Why? I didn't have a say in the matter, so I suffered (in the way middle class first world homes can suffer...) and was unhappy about it. If my parents had even given me 10% of what they saved on their heating bill, man I would have probably cranked that thing down till 0 until the pipes froze. So it's important to make sure personal no'ing comes with a reward.

What could this reward be? Anything that motivates you - this is about your happiness and not being in crippling debt or watching a savings account remain flat. Suddenly, it's easy to say no to brie in the grocery store - you're going to use whatever you save this month and put it towards an awesome vacation in winter. You let the brie go bad half the time anyway, so waste not want not.

This is what I mean about trade-offs - you balance the yes and the no, and you prioritize things based on your happiness. Whether you consciously outline your goals and budget according to achieving those goals or you're more like me and you make the rewards sweeter by saying no often, you'll find yourself doing things that matter significantly more to you if you reframe purchases in terms of trade-offs.

Of course, back to Sarah's dinner. This time around, you think of it in terms of what you want to do and what your goals are. You've done a lot of dinners and you have drunk a lot of drinks… what if you saved that money and instead took Swing lessons or went to a wine and painting class (confession: I'm a total sucker for these, if Sarah's dinner was a wine and painting class, count me in!). By reframing purchases in terms of trade-offs, you're seeing the value of your money for what it can do for you, not just a percentage of your paycheck, etc. and you also put more value on your time.

You can't always reframe things. For example, you really should not reframe your grandfather's funeral; some experiences (although not fun) can only occur once and if you don't participate, you may regret it for a lot longer than the $200 plane ticket it would cost you. I also encourage you not to live a purely hedonistic lifestyle of "woooo I only do things that entertain me". You'll find yourself burnt out and wondering why all your friends have houses and kids and fancy vacations while you make simple short term choices based on momentary happiness. Yikes!

Reframing things in terms of trade-offs is really helpful for people who struggle with long term saving. The happiness from a latte today is more meaningful and, frankly, obvious than $3.60 put towards retirement. Even if you try to calculate what that $3.60 is going to be in 40 years assuming a 6% average growth rate in the stock market, you're looking at $39.68. Woo?

However, what if I told you that you could have a latte now or a better latte later for the same amount? Or what if I told you that you could have a week of daily lattes or go to a concert on Friday? Or what if it was a year of lattes or a plane ticket to Hawaii (3 $3.60 lattes per week x 52 weeks/year = $562 whereas a plane ticket Seattle to Hawaii is like ~$450 round trip)? I bet some of you would have different answers.

I am picking on coffee a lot here, which is often the target of the "latte fallacy" [3] where people are in debt/poor because they buy lattes instead of saving. However, this applies to many things people buy every day and of which they think nothing. Do you buy the most expensive thing on the menu when you go out to eat or actively choose something cheaper or mid range? Do you drive to work instead of walk/bus/bicycle? How often do you eat out? Do you buy things on sale? Ad infinitum.

Trade-off thinkers - try to process your financial transactions with the thought "is this what I want or need?" instead of letting small, effectively meaningless purchases snowball into preventing you from living the life you want. Especially if you're already setting aside a certain amount of your income to general/house/retirement savings, then suddenly your disposable "life" expenses can be reframed in terms of the vacations you want to take or the latest iPhone you want to buy.

How to determine a good/bad trade-off

As I have mentioned before, the last thing I want for you is to become a maniacal saver who cloisters themselves away in his or her house and fears spending money of any sort. Being human (and a social one) costs money, but it has the irreplaceable benefits that include things like laughter, friends, and enjoyment. I hear these things are good for your health and mental well being.

A good trade-off is one that costs you little or no joy but you save your money. These are situations where you were going to purchase something unnecessary just because you were acting instinctively (i.e. "I'm hungry") or impulsively ("I want the purple bike!"). You can identify these situations pretty easily - ask yourself if you need it and ask yourself if the value it will give you is appropriate for its cost.

If you are starving and haven't eaten in 4 days and your only choice for food in the next 6 hours is a $300 meal, by golly that will be some of the best $300 you've ever spent in your life. On the other hand, if you're not that hungry, just a little bored, and thinking about getting $5 peanuts at the airport to munch on... ask yourself do you need it or is there a cheaper alternative (re: candy bar for $1.50)? Could you anticipate this need for munchies and maybe bring $1 peanuts from the grocery store with you next time so you reduce your spending by $4?

How do you assess a trade-off situation? Every transaction is pretty much a trade-off! Think before you spend - take a moment to pause and consider. I am an impulsive person, and I can do this, so I think all of you can too. Granted, I fall off the wagon sometimes on impulsive spending, but then I look at my credit card bill, have a small heart attack, and then redouble my efforts to try to reconsider unnecessary purchases.

Trade-off Deterrents

I have really terrible news for you - likely, your peers/friends/family will not understand nor respect your trade-off value system the way you do. The best case scenario is that your life partner jives with you completely, but even that is on par with the likelihood of finding Prince Charming. Instead, you **are** going to have to defend your choices, often, and you will probably be mocked for them occasionally. For whatever reason, American society is particularly cruel to savers (remember Mr. Scrooge?) and even your self-no'ing will not get the positive response and cheering that it deserves.

For instance, Sarah's dinner... are your BFF's Clare and Michelle really going to cheer you for not going out with them? "Wow, we're super proud of you for making financially responsible decisions that will bring you happiness even if it means you don't get to make our dinner more fun and enjoyable for us with your presence!" Oh shit, right? We're equally cruel to recovering alcoholics ("just one drink!") and people who are trying to study to get good grades ("why don't you study tomorrow night?").

It all comes back to the no'ing and your happiness. You have to say no sometimes; if you always try to say yes, you will run out of money, time, energy, and you probably won't be that happy. This is just a fact - think about how much time you've spent doing things you didn't really want to do just because someone you cared about asked you to do it with them. It's **critical** to consider the happiness of those you care about, but if you only focus on that instead of your own happiness, then do those people you're always saying yes to really care about you? Whoa, right?

Choose friends that have a similar value system to you. If you all value sailboating, then the cost both time and money-wise will make sense. Yes, you'll still have to say no often, but it will look like this "Sorry, I can't go to dinner, I'm saving up for a new sailboat". Your like-minded friends will hear "sailboat" and get excited for you. If they chide you with "it's just one dinner, it won't hurt your savings that much", you can try to improvise with "well I can order a side of fries" or "how about you all come over to watch races later at my place?". Repeat now and forever: having friends does not have to cost you (that much) money.

Also, be strong - stick to your guns. Everyone has different values and interprets money differently. Some people want to retire at 45, some people want to retire at 70... some people are in debt up to their eyeballs and others want to live debt free to the point where they will only buy a house if they can pay in full. For your own part, you can make the world a better place by encouraging your friends and family to make smart financial choices ("you saved for retirement today?! I'm so proud! Really!"). A little positive encouragement goes a long way.

5. Find opportunities that pay

My generation (Millennials) struggle(d) with choosing a satisfying career that accomplished good in the world that also compensated well enough to eat and/or afford their ideal lifestyle. I won't focus too much on the tribulations of Millennials (cough, student debt, cough), but the above issue caused a pretty clear schism in career choice for college students - pursue your "dreams" or become a Doctor, Engineer, Lawyer, or Educator.

I'm not going to advise you to pursue your dreams with abandon - that's a luxury of those who have made it and can reminisce on their "successful" past choices or for those born wealthy. I can tell you about a lot of my peers who "pursued their dreams" and ended up with enormous college debt and no career plan, some of them working the same jobs they did in high school without a college degree. Is it worth it? For some, without a doubt, yes. For others, I think they would do anything to turn back the clock and have a solid conversation with their past selves.

I'm also not going to dare to say pre-professional or bust; being a medical doctor is an admirable and challenging career worthy of respect. However, so few Pre-Med students actually end up as licensed doctors that it's worth asking if your dream of being a doctor is realizable for you? Do you have perfect grades in your science classes? Did you do well on the MCAT? What college did you go to? If the answer is not ideal, deep breaths, you still have a lot of potential to change the world in an amazing way and be a good person, it's just probably not by being a medical doctor.

So what is my advice?

First off, working hard isn't going to bring you a successful career and lots of money. Working hard is a part of a bountiful career rife with bonuses and promotions, but you could work really hard at digging a hole to nowhere in your backyard and get …
nowhere.

Next, you don't need to follow a plan to make money and have a career, but you do need to follow your strengths and consider how you can use them to make money. We all have strengths, they almost certainly have pecuniary value in some way, but it's entirely up to you to find the right way to combine them into a sustainable and profitable career path.

Example: I wanted to be a doctor, I thought it was my dream. I just wanted to help people, make my parents proud, and take nice vacations one day. I knew from high school I was good at Physics, Biology, Typing (yes, that's a strength), and Math. I also knew I was pretty wretched at Chemistry, but I decided to ignore all advice and follow my dreams with a Pre-Med major. I took my first Chemistry class in college, and I did awful (by doctor standards, a B). It was completely heart wrenching for me - I knew there was little hope for me becoming a doctor with those kind of grades in Intro Chemistry.

So, I limped my way over to the Physics department and declared a Physics major - it was the only thing I ever found in school to be both exciting and something at which I was good. However, at the time, I figured it was something that was so "easy", no one could possibly ever pay me to do Physics. It'd be like a degree in Philosophy, something impractical. To me, Physics seemed so intuitive that everyone had to understand it - little value there. In fact, I figured since I was going to be a "dreamer" I would also pick up another useless but interesting degree - Latin.

What started as a choice born out of failure, ended up in a dream career with infinite choices and directions of pursuit. However, this was one of the last major life choices I made purely on "passion" instead of where I wanted to go in life. I found I loved research my second year of undergraduate, and I realized that was what I wanted to be my future career - research.

From there, I figured out what I needed to succeed in a research based career in Physics. I needed a PhD, so I tailored my schedule and workload to get into graduate school. I asked questions, I worked hard, and I kept my eye on the prize. Despite what my graduate school colleagues might say, I wasn't smart enough to make it through without complete and utter focus. So, I developed this mantra every time someone asked for a time commitment: **is it fun? Is it something that will help my career? Is it something that will pay?** Because I needed to stay sane (fun), I had to stay focused to pass (career), and I had to pay the bills (pay). For me to do something, it had to satisfy two conditions: be necessary for career (like school) or involve very little of my time and satisfy at least one condition.

What did this look like in execution?

"Lois, we need you to chair this committee for the graduate research council"
Time: ☐☐☐☐☐
Good for Career: Yes

Paid: No
Fun: Nope, didn't involve my friends
Verdict: "No, sorry I don't have enough time to do this. However, I can recommend xyz"

Tutoring Physics/Teaching
Time: □□
Good for Career: Yes
Paid: Yes (!)
Fun: Sometimes. Sometimes not.
Verdict: Yes, and a lot of it.

Party with Friends
Time: □□, one evening
Good for Career: in a weird networking sense, sure
Paid: No, cost $
Fun: Absolutely
Verdict: Necessary for sanity, yes

Working at a Restaurant
Time: □□□□
Good for Career: No
Paid: Yes, and better than any other undergraduate job
Fun: Sometimes but mostly just work
Verdict: No, I had the option to do jobs that would pay and look good on my resume for graduate school

Research Project in Chile
Time: □□□□□□□□
Good for Career: Very much
Paid: Yes, and well

Fun: C-H-I-L-E in the summer, duh!
Verdict: One of the best experiences of my life, and it gave me valuable research experience and paid

What's the pattern with looking at Fun/Pay/Career with these time commitments? You can actually have it all (re: research in Chile) and you should hold out for opportunities that satisfy at least 2 of Fun/Pay/Career. You can't always follow this model - sometimes you **need** to pay the bills and you **need** to work a dead end job dishing out ice cream to do so. Use it as an experience and as motivational fuel to accomplish your goals; who knows, that ice cream job may end up being where you meet the love of your life or the basis of your memoir one day.

If you haven't found your passion yet, then you focus your time exploring and trying to discover what are your strengths and how you can leverage them. This isn't just advice for the young ones; there are people well into their 30s and 40s who haven't figured out what they want to do. Invest your time in different experiences and keep an open mind - pay attention to what you like doing and where you seem to find less resistance than others. Once you find a strength, start investing time in it and see if it's still a strength.

Sometimes you think you've found a passion (or a fun, well paying, career-focused experience) and … it's not. It's exactly like meeting a guy and thinking "he's the one" and finding out a year later while sobbing that he's "not the one" because he likes a few other women too. Try hard and fail fast when you can - immerse yourself in the experience, give it 100%, keep the open mind evaluating how you feel, and look for warning signs. We'd all love to take back relationships we were in a year too long when we knew the warning signs were there. Admit failure and rise to the next challenge - don't languish in a career that isn't meant for you out of stubbornness or because "it's your dream".

Just to make it confusing though, don't be a quitter either. This is a difficult line to toe, resilience versus stupidity. I was best at Physics, wanted to be a doctor, and did not have skills at making perfect grades and anything involving Chemistry - quitting was wise. While pursuing Physics, I was told by a Math professor that "some people (re: me) are just not that good at Math" - I turned around and got an A in the next two classes (resiliency). Fuck that dude.

There **will** be roadblocks in any career you choose, but you have to decide if those roadblocks are external or internal. External blocks are set by others based on their opinion (re: stereotype) of you. Internal blocks are in your head - either you think you can't do it or you think you lack the knowledge and/or ability to do so. There is great reward is fighting through problems and solving them, but some problems may not be worth your time and effort to conquer. Remember, digging a bottomless hole requires resiliency, but what's the point?

The other message I want to make clear is that you don't need a piece of paper that says "this person is qualified" in order to be successful. If you revile school (very few people truly like school, but this is for the people who are stunningly miserable every time they enter a classroom to the point of depression) then don't force it. There are so many ways to make money (entrepreneurship, restaurant management, construction, resource management, distribution, farming, on and on and on) and build a lasting career without getting a college degree.

Sometimes if you "force" school, you can end up worse than where you started (in debt, older, 4 years behind on your career you were already successful in when you left for school). Treat education as a job and non-paying investment in your career - you're there to find your strengths and build on them.

Alternative ways to increase income

After that massive pep talk, let's say you have a career that you are passionate about (or not, this still applies), but it doesn't pay as much as you would like. The first thing to assess is if it is a reasonable possibility for you to expend more time and energy without hurting your primary career in order to increase your capital. Then also consider if there are other ways for you to increase your take home and help your current career (Pay + Career).

This path is somewhat for the young and reckless but also for those who really want to make a difference. Sometimes the best way to come up with a startup idea is to entrench yourself in a larger company first, see what the market needs are, and then launch your own company. We can't all be Bill Gates and at 18 work out of our parents' garage and pursue an idea that leads to a multi-billion dollar company. However, by working at another job first (i.e. Firefighter) you may realize a niche need within that field (i.e. more breathable fireproof gloves) and combine that with your hobby of designing fireproof clothing.

Launching a startup is a big alternative way to increase income, but let's scale down a bit. Teaching, consulting, and training can be lucrative ways to increase your net income without using too much time. Like the paragraph before, this lies on your experience and knowledge in some subject matter that others may find valuable. It doesn't have to be related to your career either. I know a lawyer who also coaches individuals on how to perform better in bike races (she was a former pro). Although it probably pales in comparison to what she makes as a lawyer, she still is adding to her income, she loves it, and she helps others fulfill their potential. There is nothing wrong with working a side job that feels like a hobby.

Then there are small ways, basically what I like to consider "cost neutral hobbies". You sell paintings in order to buy paint supplies, you have an Etsy store where you sell soap you make at home, etc. These start as hobbies and may be the passion of your life but you recognize the likelihood of scaling out the operation into something you could support yourself on is extremely unlikely. The goal of this side income is to break even - to have your hobby pay for itself. As long as this continues to be fun and not stressful, then this side income is worthy of praise - you've made fun pay for itself!

Beyond that, you're looking at full fledged secondary jobs that may not fall heavily into the fun category, but they do increase your income and don't interfere with your primary job. This can include things like driving for Uber, Airbnb, babysitting, flipping items on craigslist, flipping houses, delivery services, working holiday shifts, and other temp/load optional work. These types of jobs are great depending on how motivated you are and how bad your financial situation is - you can work a lot of hours with uber and make decent bonus money to put towards Christmas presents, etc. Although not "fun" per se, if you see this as a choice (i.e. Chapter 1) it can be something you look forward to and a way to meet new people and gain experiences (all while getting paid!).

These types of flexi-jobs can bring in money in a meaningful way, but they don't necessarily aid your career, so it is best to proceed cautiously with how much of your time you invest here instead of on your career. Don't get me wrong, Airbnb and Uber driving can be a full-time, well paying job, but for most people it's a good side gig to afford nicer vacations, pay off their mortgage, etc.

The opposite of the flexi-jobs is what I like to call the intangibles - these may pay marginally if at all but are enormously beneficial to your career. Intangibles have a delayed payout, and it can be hard to see the benefit sometime. These include things like keeping a blog, building web pages, volunteering, etc. Intangibles feel like exactly what I'm advising you not to do, spending your free time doing things you may/may not love, but they can dramatically change your social network and unveil other opportunities down the road which are hugely advantageous.

Some careers hinge completely on intangibles - like real estate and entrepreneurship (i.e. selling wine). For example, I met my real estate agent via my bicycle race team. I knew she was someone I could trust and liked her a lot, so when I went to buy a house, she was the first person I thought of and asked to help me find a home. For Liz, being on a race team was an intangible - yes, it was a hobby she enjoyed but also being part of a team meant that she expanded her possible client base enormously. Since real estate agents spend most of their time trying to source clients, this is huge!

For my own career, I have found keeping a blog to be beneficial, especially when I am looking for a job. My blog covers many topics and isn't necessarily something I update consistently. However, it is a written history of my past and some of the projects I've finished. When potential employers are Google searching me, it comes up. Typical response? They love it - they put me on the fast track to hire because of it. Is it because my blog material is profound? Absolutely not. It's because it gives them a chance to get to know me from the comfort of their own home and in total privacy, which makes them (usually!) like me before we even get to the interview room. So even though I have spent hundreds of hours of my life writing that blog, it's turned into tens of thousands of dollars in job offers. That's a serious intangible.

Oh, and I've only made about ~$32 off the ad revenue. That definitely doesn't count as side income $32 / 200 hours = $0.16 an hour. Yippee.

Your intangibles are up to you - they can be time consuming and narrow focused (i.e. a daily Bible study) or they can be wide ranging and a minor time commitment (i.e. a monthly newsletter about feminism to a 10,000 person mailing list). You have to choose how to spend your free time, whether it's driving for Uber or joining a running team in the hopes of making meaningful connections/getting joy. However, both of these are better than staying home and watching tv every night, so I encourage you to make the most of your energy and youth!

The last point to hit in this chapter is that it's never too late to change - don't let age be a deterrent. Life's a winding journey and we're all collecting life tiles in some way... but it's not a game, there isn't a winner or loser. If you realize you're stuck and want to un-stuck yourself, rip off the bandaid and open up to new possibilities, a new hobby, and/or a new career. Please don't use that as an excuse to abandon your family or neglect commitments during a mid-life crisis, but just because you didn't go to Law School at age 22 doesn't mean you're a failure for life and can never go to law school. The path may be harder later in life for you, but it is rarely truly impossible (OK professional Football player might be impossible at age 60...). If past you didn't make the wisest education and/or career choices, current and future you are not irrevocably bound to those choices.

Go get'em tiger.

6. Investing is not only for "Smart Guys"

There are a lot of weird phobias that exist around investing your money in the stock market. After finally mentally breaking through that barrier myself, it's a real head scratcher to me why we (the common people) don't actively try to fight against those myths.

Myths? Let's talk about 5 investing myths based on fear.

Fearful Myth 1: The stock market crashes and I don't want to lose all my money and house.

Yes, it absolutely does, the fact the stock market tanks sometimes is totally indisputable.

However, the chance that you'd lose everything in a diversified stock portfolio and all of society hasn't crashed around you is effectively nil. If the stock market crashes, it will also likely take the housing market, kill the job market, inflation will rise, and society at large will tighten the belt. You, stuffing $50,000 under your mattress and calling it good, will not be immune from the stock market crash. Look at the recession of 2008 - the housing market burst and took everything down with it, causing countless people to lose their homes and jobs. Having that $50,000 under the mattress is great to pull out at your hour of need, but it isn't a bulwark against a stock market crash.

In fact, I'm going to argue it puts you at an extreme disadvantage.

Let's say you took the $50,000, invested for 6 years, and the Fortune 500 returned an average of 6% a year, which is a very typical assumed average rate over time. After 6 years, you're looking at collecting $21,664.35 in dividend return for a net total for $71,664.35 if you compound daily (which you do). So if the stock market massively crashed, it would have to crash 30.2% percent in order to be back to the original $50,000 you started with 6 years ago.

A 30% stock market drop is an economically devastating event - it **does** happen but not often. A bear market occurs when there's a 20% sustained reduction. Serious crashes (>30%) completely ruin our economy. Your 50k post crash, whether from under the bed or from stock market losses isn't going to be worth much anyway. So 6 years of reasonable GDP growth would take a super, life-destroying crash to nullify the benefits of investing.

Oh, did I mention, our government also allows you to take capital losses (what you lost when the market crashed) off your taxes? Suddenly, it's harder to justify leaving that 50k under your mattress to collect dust or in a savings account with a 0.25% annual interest growth rate. PS banks love you when you put huge amounts of money into CDs or Savings Accounts because they turn around and reinvest your "savings" into things like mortgages, etc. which get them a 4%+ interest rate in return. Cha-ching!

The way to play the stock market is to be **diverse** and to **play the long game**. If you buy individual stocks, you put yourself at risk of having to know the right time to buy/sell. If you buy small shares in thousands of stocks, it's more reflective of general market performance (re: 6% a year). There will be dips, and big ones too, but you need to just hold out and avoid selling your stocks when they're low. The worst time to sell a house is right after the housing market has crashed, so don't panic and sell everything after the economy crashes. Hold tight!

Fearful Myth #2: It's too complicated for me.

Where's the flabbergasted emoji... it's about as hard to sign up for an email account as it is to start investing. You can make it as easy or as hard as you want, but the easy stuff is very, very easy.

Let's start with the easy way.

You go to a stock broker portfolio site like Fidelity, Blackrock, Vanguard, etc. and open an account. If you're struggling with this, ask their very attentive hotline which has people who **very much want** you to get an account and invest. You then link your savings account where your $50,000 lives. Then, you navigate to where the Fortune 500 or Fortune 200 or whatever is a large mix of big company stocks are, and you buy a good chunk of it (let's say $10,000). You usually need some kind of minimum, anywhere between $500 and $10,000 (you get a better expense ratio with a larger investment usually).

Wait, what's an expense ratio? It's how much the fund manager is going to take - it's their "cut of the profits". It's usually pretty tiny, less than .1%. Shortcut: **you want this number to be as low as possible.** Buy the cheap, mix blend stuff (wow, I never thought I'd say that about anything) unless you have a particular industry you want to target, like medical, energy, etc. A good expense ratio is 0.04-0.06% but I personally have investments all the way up to .15% (above that is straight up highway robbery).

That's it - that is all it takes to start investing. You start putting away $100 or $10000 regularly and you can check the growth as much as you want. Warning - you're never going to see your money double overnight with safe and lazy investing. Based on historical averages, you'll see about 6% a year (but that means some years are negative - my first year of investing was!). So if you invest $1000 and let it sit for a whole year, you may have ~$1060 after a year. Not a huge difference, but this investing game is really all about compound interest and the long game.

This is so easy to do and start saving, I am going to shame you here if you haven't dropped this book and opened a Fidelity or Vanguard account. Seriously, people younger (and less intelligent) than you have figured it out and people way older (i.e. my grandma) have managed to open such an account when they struggle to remember their computer password. Stop making excuses and go do it.

The idea behind index funds stemmed from John C. Bogle's 1951 undergraduate thesis at Princeton [4]. His research showed that most mutual funds underperform when compared to money invested in broad stock market indexes. Even when selected individual stocks do beat the index funds, management fees reduced the net profit back to the investor to below the total profit of the index funds.

The Vanguard cornerstone index fund (VFINX) takes the 500 largest US companies (which account for ¾ of the US stock market value, astoundingly) and slices them into microshares that they sell to you [5]. For instance, if you want to invest $15, you can't buy a full share of Amazon stock (>$1000 a share). Instead, you would buy a partial share from a broker (who sells partial shares to other people too). Vanguard serves as your broker here and instead turns your $15 into 500 tiny (and not necessarily equal) investments in the Fortune 500 companies.

Now, the harder way.

Typically when we've read about the stock market, it's in terms of individual stocks, not a pile of them sliced together into fractional shares that we buy from an index fund manager. We hear about mysterious stock brokers who know how to get 20% gains from the market (holy shit!). You pay them a commission and they buy "the right stocks" for you and you win. There is no guarantee that an excellent stock broker will have continued success, but they spend all their time doing research and trying to choose the best individual stocks for their clients. Look at a few interviews with Warren Buffet, the ultimate stock broker (working for himself) - he is obsessed. You pay them for this service though, and it's far more than a 0.05% expense ratio.

I personally choose not to go the stock broker route - this seems like the ultimate laziness to me. I think for comparable laziness to the index fund approach, you pay more for a stock broker or financial advisor and there is more potential risk (also more potential gain). The idea of trusting one person that much bothers me; can you imagine being 50 and have your entire retirement and future hinging on the decisions of one person who isn't … you?! I get they might be an expert but an expert in guessing the future?

However, doing your own research and investing in individual companies… this I can respect. This is a lot of work with high risk but high reward potential. I know several Millennials who have done this and fared very well with targeted early investments in companies that then grew 100% within a year (hand claps). You can also temper risk a bit too by making large investments in big (re: slow moving) companies that you think may grow substantially in the next year.

The smart thing to remember with individual stock purchasing is to diversify and spread for success. If you only own Tesla stock and it emerges that engines on the new Model S spontaneously combust after 3 years, then you're in trouble and could see a massive loss. If you own Tesla, McDonald's, and Walgreens stock, the loss would be somewhat mitigated. High risk can have a high pay off, like owning Amazon stock in the 90s, but it's just wiser to make sure you spread the risk around a bit.

What I do

I'm a low risk and fairly lazy person; I buy the Vanguard 500 index fund (expense ratio 0.05%) and occasionally mix in some bonds and international stocks just to diversify, but I keep these closer to 5% of my total investment. I also keep some individual company stock (Microsoft and Facebook) because I worked for these companies and believe in their future. That's the whole of my investing - I have a phone app that I check once a week or so on how I am doing.

Now, some of you are reading that and going "you lost so much money not doing ... xxx". Yes, yes I probably did. It's amazing how clear the past is and how obvious our less optimal choices are. I am a low risk, lazy person though and I would argue most people are like me - they want something that history convincingly shows will beat inflation and grow with time. Call it investing for those who believe in steady compound interest (and dummies).

So is that really too complicated for you? I think too much of you as one of my readers to believe that.

Fearful Myth #3: It will complicate my taxes

I can't even believe I have to address this. Are you all not using Turbo Tax or freetaxusa.com? Your index fund/stock broker will give you the forms you need when you cash out your stockpiles of stock. You turn over these forms to Turbo Tax, which will take the numbers from the appropriate boxes, cue some math, and give you out the number of dollars you owe (or should get back).

Also, in some cases, it will simplify your taxes. Capital gains, which are your return on what you invested (not the base you invested initially - you've already paid taxes on that!) are taxed at a flat 15% rate (subject to income bracket, but mostly 15%, if your income tax rate is less than that, then it's 0%). For most of you, that is a lower tax rate than your income tax bracket. This should also make you outrageously mad that someone who collects stock market dividends to the tune of >$1,000,000 a year pays their taxes at a lower rate than you do. Hrmpf.

You also don't pay capital gains taxes until you sell the dividends on your shares. If you sell the principal, then you don't get hit with taxes (woo! Well... don't get hit with taxes *yet*).

I've certainly dated men who are far more complicated than doing my taxes with investments. I guess with the above logic in the title, I should stop dating men. However, I can think of a lot of reasons I'll continue to date men (life fulfillment, being attracted to them, they can open jars, etc.). By now, you also know there are a lot of reasons to invest (compound interest, cha-ching!) so... if you're going to date men (or women!), you should also invest (bam, logic).

Fearful Myth #4: I don't have enough money to invest

You probably don't; hey, I can call a spade a spade when I see it. You probably live paycheck to paycheck and if you lost your job, it would be devastating if not impossible to recover from the gap in paychecks. Money seems to flow in and back out as soon as it comes in.

Well, you've read Chapter 1 and 2 at this point, you know my response is going to be that you have to make it work because you just do. With the same irrefutable logic, I'm also going to tell you that you do have enough money to invest.

An app called Acorns recently came out that made investing your spare change easy [6]. It's a brilliant concept really - set up people's bank accounts to round up when they make a purchase and then take the "spare change" and put it towards buying blended stock portfolios. You pay $1/month for this service and start investing in the stock market 37 cents at a time; still don't have enough money to invest?

Without looping back to the previous half of this book, it's important to realize that saving in whatever way you can and putting that money away is critical for your success in realizing your long-term goals and for your happiness. You need to do this in whatever way works best for you - whether it's taking it out of your paycheck immediately or using an app that charges you ridiculous expense ratios but takes your spare change and puts it in a meaningful piggy bank.

Here are a few of my suggestions for investing when you don't have any money to save:

- Every time you get a monetary gift, unexpected windfall, or reward, split it in half. Half goes to you treatin' yo self and half goes to savings

- Yeah, use that Acorns thing to invest your spare change

- Take a certain amount of money out of your paycheck every month and invest it. Can be as little as $10!

- Anytime you can say "no" to a purchase you were going to make but resisted, take a fraction of its value and invest it.

- Sell some of your possessions (clothing, books, toys, etc.) and put half the money towards investing

- Get a side job that is only a few hours of work a week and use some of that money for investing

- Challenge a friend in a similar financial situation to invest with you and see how much each of you can save toward investments in a month.

Note: I put "half" towards investing multiple times above - why? Because getting burned out from saving is a real thing and you end up going back to your previous poor spending habits (or develop new ones). Make life fun and happy by balancing your responsibility with reward, and I think you'll find you look forward to investing and saving.

Fearful Myth #5: I will think about retirement later when I am (fill in blank here).

I think one of the problems with starting to get into a saver's mentality is that when you hear "I am saving for…" you expect the completion of that phrase to be "retirement". Let's not kid ourselves, the idea of retirement is straight up laughable in your 20s when you can barely scrape it together for the security deposit on an apartment or even get a job.

Saving for retirement feels like going to an annual doctor's appointment - it costs you money, it's not exactly fun, and at age 25 there doesn't seem to be a lot of point. Of course, if you have a rare but treatable blood disorder, you may feel like skipping on the doctor's appointments was a misstep later. And, I can almost assure you, you will regret not saving for retirement earlier.

The first major reason to start saving for retirement at a young age is compound interest. The compound interest **should** be obvious at this point - a few thousand now ends up being a few tens of thousand way down the road (quick math for you - 6% a year on $1000 means you pretty much double your principal in ~11 years with daily compounded interest).

Never fear, that's not the only reason - otherwise why lock your saved money into "retirement" instead of keeping it flush for great investments like a boat or really fancy car?

Reason 2 is that the US government really wants to incentivize people saving for retirement so they don't have to deal with millions of elderly, unable to work individuals who have nothing to live on at the end of their lives. Squirreling away for retirement is the most significant way to save on your taxes as a single individual who is working a first job and doesn't have kids or a house, especially if you don't make that much money.

Take a deep breath, we're going to go through it all.

There are two types of IRAs (individual retirement accounts). The Roth IRA is more important to young, poorer people. The premise of the Roth IRA is no major tax break now, but you will reap the gains when you withdraw in retirement by paying **no capital gains** (capital gains = 15% tax rate). That's right - you start putting away money in your 20s, you let it grow 40 years (remember it doubles about every 11) and wowza, you're looking at a x8 on your original investment and you don't pay any taxes on that increase. None. The "catch" with the Roth IRA is that you pay income taxes on your income currently (don't worry, it's already taken out of your paycheck, you don't have to pay anything else when you put your money into an IRA).

I made hay with the Roth IRA while I was in graduate school. I was at approximately a 10% tax rate (yay making below the poverty line in Michigan) and so "paying taxes now" was a minimal burden I had already resigned myself to it. However, I will let it sit and compound with time... putting a x8 on my base principal - $15,000 will likely become ~$120,000 by the time I retire. That means I will save over $15,000 in taxes when I withdraw the whole sum to travel Italy extravagantly for several years. Holy smokes - that was the amount I originally put in!

The other type of IRA, the Traditional IRA, behaves identically to a 401 k (more discussion there later). The Traditional IRA (dude, I don't make these names) allows you to take whatever you invest that year off your income taxes. So you invest $3000? $3000 comes off your total income; so if you're in the 25%-30% bracket, the Traditional IRA starts looking like the better investment because you get 30% of it back to reinvest or buy yourself something nice with. Sweet deal!

There's another added benefit to being particularly indigent but still somehow saving for retirement. The government **will** give you a fraction back of what you save for retirement. Yes, you read that correctly - the government will give you FREE money for saving for retirement if you make below $64,000 in 2018. The benefit you're looking for is called the "Saver's Credit" [7] and it means you can get up to $2,000 back from the government for putting money into an IRA or an employer sponsored retirement plan. That's $2000 a year FOR FREE to save. FOR FREE. There is some fine print to it, like you can't be a full-time student or someone else's dependent, but other than that... it's free money back to you for saving.

Ah, one catch to both types of IRAs - there are investment limits. You can only invest up to $5500 (more if you're older) a year. For the first few years I saved for retirement, I never hit the $5500 goal, I hit more like $800 but hey, that's certainly better than nothing. The other limit is that you can only invest in government sponsored IRAs if you make less than a certain amount of money. The Roth and Traditional IRAs start to phase out at about 135k for single individuals in 2018 [8].

Remember that whole discussion of why you need to save before you make big money? There's a sweet spot of time in life and income for saving for retirement where the government is going to try to massively help you out and taunt you with free money. If you wait till you make $200k a year, first you'll be paying 30%+ in taxes on it and second, any incentive to save for retirement will have to come from you. Everyone's already going to assume that you're rich enough and should be able to save on your own.

Another advantage to being young with a Roth/Traditional IRA - house buying. Once again, somehow the politicians agreed that it's a tough pill for young people to swallow to put their money in a Roth/Traditional IRA and have all these "penalties" you're hit with if you withdraw from your IRA before 65 (you have to pay income tax on your interest gains for Roth and your principal for traditional plus a little extra; not devastating but certainly annoying). So, they put some exceptions in there, like house buying. If you want to buy your first house, you can use your IRA as part of the down payment without tax liability; yep, that's right again, the government is incentivizing you to save for a house. Wow!

So the question is why aren't you saving for retirement at this point? You can use it for a house, you can pull it out and use it in case of emergencies, and if somehow you manage to never touch it, you're going to be really well set up later in life. The earlier you start, the more pronounced the returns and benefits are, even if you don't invest the full $5500. There's a definite mental comfort to having a large pile of money that you could potentially draw from any time you really needed it throughout your life - but you have to start somewhere to build it up.

Besides magical IRAs, there are a few other ways to save for retirement where there's a "free money if you do this" incentive. 401ks, which sound like some kind of robot, are employer sponsored retirement accounts. Government rules are you can contribute up to $18,500 a year (wow) and usually your employer kicks in something to encourage you to save. A common one is your employer will match up to a certain percentage of your contribution. For example, your employer may match 50% of what you contribute, which would be ~$9,000 on a $18,500 annual contribution. This would bring you to a total of ~$27,500, holy mackerel!

401ks aren't just free money from your employer either, they work just like Traditional IRAs. The money you contribute (just you, not your employer's additions) are taken off your taxable income. If you make 100k a year and you squirrel away 18k into your 401k then the government considers your taxable income to be 82k a year. That means you're saving an additional several thousand dollars a year in taxes just by doing what you should be doing anyway - living below your income and saving money for the future.

Two catches to the 401k: first is that you sometimes don't get to control what you're investing in (gasp!). Sometimes employers want you to invest in their stock specifically. This can be risky - suddenly not only does your job depend on your employer but so does your retirement; if your company goes under, you're screwed in more ways than one. It's important for you to get all of the information first and make sure it's a good investment for you.

The second is that your employer may not match or contribute anything. 401k matching is a gift, not a requirement. An example of a not-so-great 401k - the first company I worked for out of school was a small startup. They offered no 401k matching and they required you to invest in their "special blend" of stocks which was a reflection of their top customers. So even with the massive tax break, I decided that it wasn't really the right choice for me and instead I channeled the extra money I had into saving for a house. Do I regret it? Maybe a smidge, my taxes were high that year; but then again, I did get a lot farther ahead on saving for a house because of that decision.

All three (Traditional IRA, Roth IRA, and 401k) involve putting the money you save in some sort of investment portfolio. For Traditional and Roth IRAs, you get to choose and I recommend you choose something that is going to be fairly low risk and grow reliably with time. Your money is going to (hopefully) be sitting there a while. For the 401k, as mentioned above, sometimes you get to choose. Do your research!

My advice? Go for maxing out your Roth IRA as soon as you can and start contributing to it as you read this (put that latte money in your Roth IRA!). I like the Roth IRA max out when you're young because of the tax benefit on the compound interest (cha-ching!)

From there, look at your 401k (if you have one) and consider what your employer matching is, what your tax rate is, and what are your other immediate savings goals. Maxing out savings for retirement is not always the right answer; investing in your own company (re: a startup) or buying a house are significant financial investments that may have greater net gains for you in the long run than saving for retirement. However, not saving for any of the above isn't OK!

7. Debt sucks

Debt just sucks, there's no sugarcoating it. My cute anecdote about debt is that I realized how "devastating" personal debt was around the age of 8. My parents gave me a monthly allowance of my age in dollars per month if I completed my chores. My brother, fiscally responsible in the extreme even as a young child, always had superfluous cash floating around - he seemed to be able to float along just fine on what he was given.

Me, on the other hand, would blow through my allowance in 2-3 days. In fact, it was so bad that my parents started letting me "borrow" on my next month's allowance. Allowance day would come and instead of 8 dollars, I'd get $5 (and it'd be gone - I needed a new yo-yo!) and back in debt again. I even descended into shark loan territory when my brother started offering to front me money at a small charge. My parents were genuinely worried I would be like this as an adult - completely impulsive and never having two pennies to rub together.

Even my 8-year-old tiny mind hated this process. My brother was able to buy the big lego sets, etc. whereas I never could save for anything I wanted. Things like Christmas were agonizing for me - I knew my mom wanted the pink sweater but I could only afford to get her a pencil (times were tough).

I didn't break the endless-debt cycle until I was 15 (a late bloomer on many things). I wanted a Sedu hair straightener very badly to try to help my teenage self-confidence a bit, but they cost $150 apiece. I had never had more than $50 to my name at any given time, let alone $150... but I saved. I guess this is when I learned Chapter 1 and 2 - I started saying no to things and focusing on the hair straightener fund. When I bought it (cleaning out my bank account...), it was one of the most gratifying feelings. Even though I don't straighten my hair anymore, I have kept that hair straightener with me as a relic - breaking out of the hopeless debt cycle.

Many of you, I'm sure, wish your debt problems could be solved by a $150 saving project and a hair straightener at the end. Student loans are horrible, especially if you aren't in the "extremely lucrative" job you'd thought you'd be in at the end of college. Honestly, my words here can offer little comfort to the $10,000 or $100,000 you may owe Sallie Mae (shudder) right now.

Let's talk about the different kinds of debt you're likely to have in your 20s and some thoughts on how to manage it. The sad reality is that you may not get to "solve" your debt problems in your 20s, but you can put yourself on track to getting out of debt and on with your real estate empire instead of exacerbating the situation.

Student Loans

Student loans do not need to be the end all be all of your life. It's not even the most horrible nor frustrating kind of debt to have on hand, really. Poking around the Sallie Mae site, which is one of the most aggressive and frustrating loaners, you can get fixed rates of about 5.7% as of November 2018 [9]. What does that mean? Well, it's the same as that 6% stock market growth thing above except this one works against you and in favor of Sallie Mae.

5.7% isn't awful, really. Inflation is approximately 2% a year, so you're really paying Sallie Mae 3.7% for the privilege of a massive, massive loan to an individual who has no way of backing the loan or even a job to pay it back at the time when the loan was issued. 5.7% also isn't horrible as far as paying back - you're going to be able to do this, it just will take time, patience, and effort.

Student loans fall into the category of non-critical debt - you can take your sweet time in paying these off. You may **want** to pay off your student debt slowly in order to focus on investments and buying a house in the short-term; if we're in a strong stock market with 10% growth, you're going to be net richer by investing in the stock market instead of paying off your student loan debt. Think about it - $1000 of debt with 5.7% interest is $1058.65 compounded daily. Instead, if you use that $1000 and invest with market returns of 10.1%, then you're at $1106.26. You gain $47.61 by investing in the stock market that year instead of paying off your debt. Wild.

You can't predict the stock market, though, so a better way to manage student loan debt is to steadily and consistently pay it off - never stop. Honestly, before you imagine yourself in chains for 30 years paying off this debt, it's kind of that way with everything in life. Even once you own your house, you still have to pay taxes on it every month. The bills will never stop, so it's best just to learn how to deal with several spinning plates at once.

Full disclosure - I didn't have student debt. Don't hate me, it wasn't exactly easy for me either. My parents covered tuition and helped offset some living expenses, but I did work several jobs in college to make sure I could cover rent and other expenses. I ate a lot of ramen and said a lot of no. However, I have observed enough friends' and boyfriends' debt management to tell you what works and what doesn't.

Things that don't work

Completely ignoring your debt and pretending that it isn't there. Remember how in 11 years at 6% growth, you'll double the value of your principal? Yeah, that's true of student loans too. I had a boyfriend who just went "la la la I'll pay off my loans later", and he bought a nice car and took some nice vacations instead. He kept telling himself I'll pay off that $15,000 later when I have a better job. $15,000 is very little student debt, relatively speaking for an engineer, but you can imagine his surprise when 4 years later, he checked his debt and instead of between $15,000-$16,000 like he was expecting, it was greater than $20,000. Don't ignore your debt - keep an eye on it.

The other extreme, trying everything in your power to pay it off as quickly as possible, doesn't work either. Your student loan debt is likely non trivial (otherwise, wouldn't it be gone already?) and you're probably going to have to pay it off in small to mid-size installments over years. Setting an expectation to pay it off $50,000 in 3 months is not only unreasonable but for most, completely impossible. Don't give yourself impossible goals with your student loans - the aim here is to beat them not let them beat you.

I wish this one was a joke, but refinancing your loans in a way that makes them worse is also a wrong way to deal with student loans. I do know at least one person who refinanced their loans in a way to give themselves more money available now (which wasn't necessary) but a higher interest rate. Don't do this unless you really are starving to death, otherwise go back and re-read Chapter 2 on how what you have is enough!

Things that do work

The mantra of student loan repayment should be "steady, iterative, reasonable payments until the debt is gone". It's really that simple - if you make $5000 a month, you think you can save $2000 a month after expenses, pick somewhere between $500 - $1500 a month to put towards your student debt and keep doing so until it's gone. This is part of the reason car payments and mortgages are set up this way too.

Another great way to repay your student debt - start making payments while still a student. This gets you used to the feeling of paying off your debt and helps you keep an eye on it. It also makes you appreciate the value of your degree more (less party more study). Plus, most of your interest is deferred until after college, so you are making payments before interest starts coming due. Your payments don't have to be much at all - even $25 a month is a solid start, and the idea is just to get you used to paying off the loans in a manageable and steady fashion.

Once you have established this regular payment plan, your next goal is to lower your interest rate as often as you can; this is refinancing. It's magical in some ways, basically another group is willing to give you a loan that will repay your current loan in full (take that Sallie Mae!) and on your new shiny loan they'll give you a lower interest rate. You're not going to see any massive changes except your accumulated interest will be lower. That's money in the bank for you!

Why should you refinance "often" (re: every 1-2 years)? Because your situation changes and you become (hopefully) a safer loan investment, so investors are more likely to give you a lower interest rate. Let's put it in perspective - who wants to give an 18-year-old a 100k loan in an unknown specialty with no college degree at that point and no loan down payment? Terrifying! No! Who wants to give a marketing professional who has an income of 120k a year, has two years of working experience, and has already paid down 30% of the original 100k loan? Ooooh, me, me! Pick me! I'll give you 4% instead of Sallie Mae's 5.7%! Your credit score, income, working experience, and debt to income ratio matter in refinancing.

Many people don't refinance because it takes work and it's not the path of least resistance. Don't be this person!! Compound interest can be your foe as much as it is your friend. Shop around - talk to a few banks (just walk in and say you're interested in refinancing) and get a few quotes on the interest rate they want to charge you. Get a few offers, play them against each other, and see how low you can go. Emphasize your stability, etc. Banks love safe bets.

The last piece of advice I can offer on this front is to do your best to change your mentality on student loans. The initial loan given to you was a necessary investment - you learned, you grew, and you now have a valuable skill set to offer society and are (hopefully but not always) using. Even if you aren't using your specialized knowledge from your major, college degrees are still valuable and often required in many careers. You need to pay back this awesome gift (huge loan to effectively a child) you were given, and it will feel like a horrible burden at times.

The only reason that my brother and I emerged from college without student debt is that my father believed it was critical for parents to pay for their children's tuition because his mother had done that for him. To be honest, it was an absurd goal for his income bracket, basically requiring him to pay a second mortgage for 20 years. He made us promise that we would do this for our children - a pay it forward model.

What my parents sacrifice meant is that I was able to put 30% down on a very expensive house 2 years after school. But it also means that I have researched 529s and how much a college tuition will cost me if I have children. I, like you all, will have a $500+ monthly payment towards a college fund for 18 years per child. I like this model more because it feels like I am giving a gift of freedom and choice rather than feeling trapped by my previous self's decisions, but it's still really expensive either way.

So maybe if you're feeling ambitious and bitter about having college debt, consider paying ahead for your child's college education after you pay off your own student loans. As much as I wish the US government would get on board with subsidized college education, I am not sure it's going to happen in my children's lifetime. Best case scenario, they do and I can turn that 529 in a series of spectacularly amazing vacations for our family. Worst case, my children get to go to college.

House Mortgages

This one is extremely contingent on where you live. If you're in NYC, "buying a house" in your 20s is comparable to saying "Watch me teleport!" and "I'm unbelievably rich and probably not from my own efforts!". If you're in rural Tennessee, well, buying a house is just kind of what you do when you're ready to make financial sense and live in one place for more than a year or two.

Buying a house with a mortgage is the best kind of debt (it still sucks though!). With a mortgage, you feel like every payment is going to "ownership" and it vaguely feels like a financial investment. Your house is (hopefully) growing in value every year, and every month a part of your payment goes to interest and a part goes to the principal. The faster you pay it down, the less you'll pay in interest. You also now have a reliable place to live where the owner (re: you!) is not going to raise your rent every year (woo!).

The additional bonus to house debt is that you can take the interest payments off your taxes up to a certain extent (meaning if your mortgage is up to $1,000,000 for an individual) [10]. This ends up being thousands of dollars sometimes, which is huge! In my case, I can make a "bonus" mortgage payment with my tax return on interest just from the house. Once again, the federal government wants people to buy houses (stability, easier for government planning, etc.), so they encourage it!

Compared to the other kinds of debt we talk about, mortgages are dirt cheap. In Fall of 2018, the national mortgage interest rate was approximately 4%. If we're figuring you are going to get about a 6% return on your stock market portfolio investments, then... you're winning by 2% to not pay off your mortgage. In fact, you're bonus winning because the mortgage interest is coming off your taxes. Major cha-ching.

So far so good, but why do house mortgages suck? Because they are attached to the house buying process. Unlike other loans, getting a mortgage comes with an excessive amount of red tape and $$$. A mortgage isn't really as good of a deal as it may seem initially because you have to front a ton of money and a good chunk of it goes down the drain too (to real estate agents, escrow charges, etc.). When I got my mortgage, they charged me $120 to simply sign the final house paperwork, in addition to countless other fees for "assessments" and "underwriting surcharges".

In order to buy a house too, you have to front the dreaded down payment. There are a lot of ways to buy a house (FHA financing, VA loans), but the standard way is a 20% down payment (at least). So on a 200k house, you need to front 40k in addition to the "closing costs" and what not. That's a lot of money to tie up in one investment, particularly if your total net worth is like 60k. If you end up losing your job and can't make mortgage payments, unless you can rapid fire sell your house, the bank will foreclose on you and **take** your house and down payment. If you're foreclosed on, that means you lose the 20% you put down and you don't have a home.

That should sound terrifying to you because it is. If I personally have a rough year and lose my job, my Vanguard funds can be liquidated in small or large quantities to float me during my year of need. At the end of the year, I'd probably still have money left over in addition to relatively maintain my way of life (not indefinitely maintainable but you get the picture). Moral of the story: don't buy a house with **all** of your money - make sure that you have enough left over for emergencies and for the sake of diversifying your investments.

There are many smarter people than myself who have come up with magic ratios of how much your mortgage payment should be compared to your net income. I can say this: 50% is really high - if you can only get a house that requires you to make monthly payments that high, think about taking on a renter or putting a room on Airbnb. Also, if you find yourself toeing the line on housing affordability, be very careful. Foreclosure happens to real people (about half a million homes during a good financial year) [11]. Foreclosure will also ruin your credit score; it's definitely not a good back up plan.

Other than that little piece of terror, buying a house is a huge positive in your life and should be seen as a major accomplishment. Whether it's a house in San Francisco or in rural Tennessee, in my eyes once you've bought a house, you're laying down a foundation for a stable financial future. House mortgage debt is "easy" debt in a way, but it needs to be treated with caution because it is so massive (100,000s of dollars in many cases).

Credit Card Debt

Now this one... the dreaded credit card debt. You **absolutely** need to get **rid of that shit** as soon as possible. Seriously, triage your situation and mitigate immediately - credit card debt will ruin you fast.

How dire is your situation? Credit card interest rates are typically between 15-20% but can get as high as 24%. Remember that 6% growth rate (it's getting obnoxious now, right?) ... yeah, if your APR is 15% that means you're losing 9% now annually by not having that money in the stock market. 9%! And if it's 24% then you're losing 18%!! My heart be still!!

Why are credit card interest rates so high? Because they are meant to be short term loans for anyone and everyone whenever you want one. Also, they're high because of the bankruptcy risk. You want to buy a new dining room table but only have $200 in your bank account? No problem! Magic credit card will give you that table! And it will only charge you your APR/12 months times the amount you owe for every month. So little for getting that table now! For example, $1000 principal only collects about $20 of interest a month (when the APR is 24% - that's 2% a month). The credit card company gives you a "minimum payment" of $20; once again, nothing!

Of the many problems with credit cards, part of the problem is the mentality along this line of thinking. It becomes "cheap" to buy things early and pay them off later; except the problem is that we didn't have the money to pay for the item(s) this month, why should we assume we're going to have the money to pay for item(s) next month? In a lot of cases, people don't pay off their credit card debt, they just keep increasing the principal amount owed until they can't afford to even pay the interest they owe.

At that point, you, innocent table buyer now with a new Mercedes and some fancy clothing to boot, are at the end of your line and stare down bankruptcy. Do you want to declare bankruptcy? Absolutely not - talk about a scarring experience that will screw you for years after you've cleaned up your financial situation. It will be hard for you to rent an apartment, it will be hard for you to buy a car with an auto loan, and if you do try to buy a house, your mortgage rates will be higher. Why? Because you're a risk now, and banks like safe bets.

Don't be ashamed if you have credit debt, tens of millions of Americans are with you [13]. It's a bad financial choice, you know it's a bad financial choice, so let's talk about fixing it.

First triage: try to do a balance transfer or talk to a bank about a short term loan (yes, the whole bank talking thing again!). A balance transfer means you negotiate with the credit card company on the interest rate you're at -

"Hey credit card company, you're great and all, but I'm trying to pay this off but the rate is pretty astronomical. Can we drop it in half? Thanks!"

That surprisingly... works. Actually. The credit card companies would rather have you pay back some of what you owe them (cutting rate in half) than none of what you owe them (bankruptcy). They also recognize that, depending on your credit score, if they won't cut your rate in half, the banks will be more than willing to give you a short term loan at a nice 9% (more or less). From the previous sections in this chapter, you all should know how cushy 9% sounds to a bank; they're only collecting 4% on your house payments!

Both of these approaches involve talking to people, but they usually work and very much to your benefit. Even though $20/month doesn't seem like a lot, cutting that down to $10/month can mean the difference between $200 or $100 in 10 months. Still doesn't seem like that much? That table only cost $1000; paying interest on it for 10 months means you've paid 20% of the value to the credit card company and have paid (still) for none of the table. Don't do this!! Don't be lazy - go call the credit card company and/or the bank.

Second triage: you need to acknowledge that you are living beyond your means if you are in sustained credit card debt and you **need** to change your lifestyle. Oof this is a hard one; the first stage of grieving is denial, right? If you've had to turn to credit cards to pay for things and you are in debt, then you are living beyond your means. Even if it was a really bad, freak situation that brought you into credit card debt, that still means you were living close to the edge and, therefore, beyond your means.

The desperate edge to this is that you can't sustain credit card debt, even if you don't want to change. You may love your life and everything about it but it's simply not a sustainable life plan. You're either just (A) making interest payments but slowly accumulating more debt or (B) paying off debt and acquiring more which means that you're paying an exorbitant amount of interest when you could have just budgeted better. Neither of those is remotely good for you and both necessitate change. The sooner the better!

The third method of triage is to take aggressive action. Unlike student debt and house mortgage, this one has got to go ASAP. Even if you have a short term loan of 9%, that's still a crazy high interest rate. There are entire books and some great YouTube videos dedicated to helping you get out of debt, but the short of it is put aside some cash for an emergency fund (1-2 months of rent) and then go gun-ho on getting rid of your debt. Sell stuff, take up a second job, cut costs, downsize, etc. - do it, you need to get out of credit card debt.

The other side to aggressive action if you think it is hopeless for you to pay whatever you owe back - declare bankruptcy. This should not be the first course of action because it's going to make life difficult for you on the other side as you rebuild. However, it is sometimes absolutely necessary. If you make 60k a year and you're 200k in credit card debt (who gave you that kind of limit, I don't know!) then bankruptcy is a must; you can probably never pay that off with the amount of interest you'd still have to pay, even with a short term loan. Bankruptcy is going to make it difficult for you to buy a house, buy a car, and even find a place to rent, so use this method only as a last resort.

After you get out of debt, you're going to be in a period of transition. Suddenly, you won't have these massive payments to make every month and this all consuming focus on getting out of debt. If you can maintain a similar lifestyle to what you have been doing while getting out of debt, you're going to have more money and be able to save, easily! Yay!

My advice: start using that surplus for savings - start a Roth IRA and start putting money into the stock market. That way, when you find yourself in a similar situation (i.e. car needs repair) it won't put you in throes of credit card debt. Instead, you'll be able to reach into your savings and fix the problem. Much, much, much less stressful.

8. Marry the (Financial) Love of Your Life

I confess I'm not the expert here since I haven't been married. However, I **could** have easily been married to several of my exes and the relationship would have still ended up the same, which is not married anymore. Several of my relationships failed because of discrepancies in how we viewed finances, and I know many couples also split for similar reasons. Unfortunately, you don't "usually" have a money discussion in a relationship until 3-6 months in, and by then, you're already attached (or in some cases, already engaged).

I do not know why philosophy on money isn't a discussion topic on a first date. You know, just shove it in right next to the questions about hobbies: "So you like running? Me too! Hey how do you feel about 401ks and real estate investments? Do you have credit card debt?". This is what can make or break an otherwise great relationship.

Why? Marriage isn't just for having children - without a prenup, you're binding yourself financially, better or worse!, to another person. Did you get married without knowing they have 60k of credit card debt? Guess what, that's now **your** debt! Legally! Yikes!

Although you may want to have that white dress party with all your friends, marriage is actually a financial (and re: non-romantic) decision. Even more unfortunate, divorce is usually a financial decision. According to a 2009 research study on divorce, one of the best indicators of marital stress is "financial disagreements". Couples that had arguments over finances are over 30 percent more likely to get divorced than couples that report disagreeing about finances a few times a month [14].

Why does money ruin great partnerships? Because money = choice = freedom. If you have money, you have choices and therefore the freedom to work, not work, buy a bicycle, buy a car, etc. Money is a critical part of the way we define ourselves - whether you choose to buy a designer handbag, go on an exotic vacation, etc. So imagine when one of the tools you use to define yourself is limited by another person? The part of the brain that maintains identity acts as a guard dog, so triggering it sends a flood of bad feelings.

There are a million different reasons why financial fights matter. If your husband believes that you should all should start saving in your 50s for retirement and vacation your little hearts out in your 30s, but you feel like you'd rather retire 5 years sooner and put your kids through college... those are some pretty major differences. Obviously, you're not going to break up because of it - "yeah Cheryl, he just lives a more hedonistic present life than I do; I mean, saving 7% instead of 17%? Hmpf - it was totally unacceptable" "OMG Jeanne, you're better off without him".

Financial loggerheads, though, is a serious problem that builds resentment and frustration over time. It's straight up toxic. Watching your savings account dwindle is very stressful for some people, and you may find yourself quibbling over stupid things like getting sweet potato fries instead of regular potato fries ("we can't afford retirement because of your damn fries!"). Fights become more barbed, and unless sacrifices to the altar of compromise are made, you will, somehow, find yourself in a toxic relationship all because of ... money!

So money does matter in a romantic relationship... a lot. Try to find someone who thinks about money with a similar value system to you - it'll make your marriage infinitely easier. Besides a similar value system though, you also need to develop a joint financial management plan. There seem to be three categories of couple financial-dom: one takes charge, both individuals remain independent, and working together. Which do you and your partner fall into?

One person takes charge and gives the other person boundaries to operate within.

Always fascinating to watch this one in play. Effectively, one person becomes the money manager of the relationship. It's generally the more frugal person (we can only hope) and typically the man in the relationship. They determine how much the couple should be saving for retirement, how much goes towards house down payment, and how much goes to food/clothing/etc. Usually, each person keeps a fraction of their paycheck for personal expenses but the net total is managed by the "boss".

I have been the "boss" in a relationship, and there are some people who are genuinely happy taking a backseat on financial matters. It takes a lot of the stress out of their life, and if you trust someone completely (like many people trust their spouses), then they can rest assured that their champion has done due diligence and their financials will be secure. This model can result in very little to almost no fighting over money matters.

That being said, I can't recommend this model. Although it works for many, I personally can't imagine putting that much faith (however blindly) to one person to always make the right choice and do what is best for us. Even if you do have that much trust, it doesn't hurt to be aware and help by offering them discussion and other lines of thinking. You may prevent mistakes, and it gives another avenue of discussion. Education is rarely a bad thing, but dependency certainly can be.

You are also completely fucked if you're the financial dependent and a divorce happens. Just saying, about ⅓ of marriages end in divorce.

Plus, saying "my husband takes care of that" is kind of lazy anyway. I get that it's nice to have "roles" within the relationship (she makes the coffee, he cleans the bathtub) but it's not a waste of time to learn and discuss investment plans. In my relationships where I've been the more "knowledgeable" one on money matters and investing, I still take the time to teach, consult, and discuss with my partner. Because that's what they are - a partner, and they have a different perspective and can help prevent bad decisions (buying expensive furniture, too expensive of a house, etc.).

If you are the boss in the relationship and find yourself not wanting to be, take the time to educate your partner. Have a discussion about how much you value their opinion and how important it is to you that they go on living their best life if tragedy strikes. It can be difficult to motivate others sometimes, but you are married to this person - you (should) know how to present investments and 401ks to them in a way that resonates. I hope.

Each member has their own plan

For more independent individuals, I think this one works well. The idea here is that each person comes into the relationship with their own financial plan and maintains that plan throughout the relationship. If you want to save for retirement instead of vacationing, then your vacation budget is smaller than your husband's and you may have to sit out a few vacations.

This plan is much more popular amongst couples on their second marriage or who are in their 40s+. They may have children that they want to provide for, they may have a retirement date in mind, and they aren't so swept up in new romance (generally...) to change their personal plan. They've been supporting themselves for a while, and they have a budget set up to do that. They are also set in their ways, not willing to readily change.

This philosophy is the antithesis of the previous plan - it's complete independence to the extreme. I can't say I particularly recommend this plan either - it's kind of two people who live together and share the same general life plan, but there is a lack of trust and/or respect for each other's personal decisions. This is the safe option - you protect yourself from the whims of another person. However, it's not really a team effort, which can cost you intimacy in a relationship.

That being said, I think the "young folk" probably should take a heavier dose of maintaining financial independence in their relationships. I think a lot of doomsday money issues in a young relationship could be solved by the two individuals entering the relationship with a plan and a sense of what matters to them, rather than trying to find that within the relationship.

For example, if you take a "la la la" approach to money and so does your partner, eventually you (will likely) hit a point where one of you is going to care (i.e. debt, raising a child, buying a house) and you'll try to craft a plan together. You may disagree - "I think we should eat out less" "well I think you should buy fewer clothes" and this is where issues can emerge.

Instead, if you both enter the relationship with a plan, then each partner in a healthy relationship has to (A) respect the other's plan in place and (B) already has their priorities ranked. That removes any potential quarrel caused by assumptions (or willful ignorance) on money matters and will leave your relationship stronger.

Growing together to come up with an Adaptable Financial Plan

OK, obviously, this is the one I'm going to heavily endorse because it means you have two (or several...) smart, capable individuals who are working together to achieve a common goal. I mean, isn't that the marriage dream? A team built on respect, empathy, and a growth mindset?

This one is challenging in execution though - it involves lots of communication, respectful discussion, and a willingness to make sacrifices to the altar of compromise. In this scenario, if one of the couple became incapable of maintaining the plan, the other member would be able to carry on "the plan" without them. Ideally, that would never happen, but no one is left vulnerable. If divorce happened, neither person could pretend that Swiss offshore account "doesn't exist".

You also are going to disagree, which is somewhat ironic because this is the "together we are strong" plan. You have to work together to come up with what works and in a successful execution, you both have space and freedom needed to make independent choices... together.

How does this version look different than option 2 - both parties are independent with their own money? In this case, everything would be a common pool and a shared bank account/credit card. You hold each other accountable. Whereas in the total independence model, the idea is that your money is your own and maybe you have some joint account you both pay into for the house. Accountability may seem like a negative thing, but I actually have immensely appreciated it in equal financial partnerships; it reduces impulsivity and keeps the focus on big goals instead of minor weaknesses (i.e. clothes).

In a dream scenario, you may also disagree over how to invest your joint money and big picture goals. One of you thinks you should invest in real estate, the other thinks you should pool your money in the energy sector - both of you have researched it and feel strongly. Although you disagree, you still have to respect the fact that the other person cares - these are not disagreements based out of selfishness or lack of empathy. When you start compromising, likely one will fold or the investments will be split in half for each one.

Why I support this option the most is that I think a couple can achieve more if they can trust each other to work together. It's part of the reason I think it's incredibly unfair when two doctors or two lawyers date - wow, what a combined salary! And when those two individuals work together... wow what a combined effort! Two people with joint goals and spending can go farther than two self accountable individuals.

Summary

Married folk and those in long term committed relationships... have the tough conversations about money. Be willing to discuss and even fight about money (amicable fight... keep it civil) - it's important, it's healthy, and it's necessary in order to keep the relationship afloat and everyone's dreams getting realized. You're a team and marriage is about every fight ending in a resolution that keeps the relationship going forward.

Figure out what works for both of you - all three options listed above are things that I have seen work in successful relationships. You may be in Option 2 and try Option 3 to only watch it blow up in your faces. This is **fine** - I mostly advocate changing your plan for couples who have zero financial plan (which doesn't work).

For those of you who haven't had the white dress party yet, have this discussion with potential partners. Ask the hard questions; you can make them fun - even "what would you do if you won the lottery?" gives you a deeper insight into what someone values. I bring it up as quickly as I can when starting a new relationship, and I haven't had anyone run for the hills yet when I ask.

In fact, usually it either turns into a test of honesty (are they in debt and willing to admit it?) or we find we have common ground and we're entering on option 2 (both individuals have a financial plan). In the case of the former, if I find out later they lied, well… if they are willing to lie about money to you, what do you think the chances are they'll lie about an affair, STD, etc.? (answer: very good).

In the case where they tell the truth and it's not good, it opens up another discussion - how did they get there and why? Do they have a plan out? Many people can be, on the surface, blasé about their debt but deep down, it's really stressing them out. This is your chance at a conversation where you find out if their plan is crazy or not, and if it is crazy, are they open to change? Very powerful things to find out early in a relationship.

I've been lucky enough to have met a boyfriend where he and I got to "live the dream" of how this conversation should go. I brought it up on the second date after a joke about college debt, with a line like "Do you have college debt?" He said he had already paid it off, quickly, after graduating. I was impressed and asked him something like "so are you still saving and investing?" and he laughed and described how he saves a lot and has fun with investing but errs conservative. Then he kind of tipped his head and with an expectation of "nothing", asked if I was saving or paying off debt. I got to smile and explain that I was a big saver, had had a Roth IRA since early graduate school, and was saving for a house ("Roth IRA" is a magical code word to indicate to other financially responsible Millennials that you have your shit together).

The look on his face after I said this flitted between shock, impressed, awe, and I think he fell in love with me at that moment. See, you didn't think it would be romantic, but knowing you aren't going to have to pay off someone's credit card debt once you're attached is a huge relief. In fact, to know that they may be as or more stable than you financially is a colossal relief. We both held hands and skipped off into the sunset after that.

Unfortunately, I ended that blossoming relationship soon after to make a series of extremely poor decisions that took me back to an ex who was the antithesis of this winner. That's why this is a book about financial responsibility, not how choose romantic relationships wisely. It also could shed some light on why I'm not married.

Anyways, the key is to have this discussion and quickly when dating. Even if it goes the other way (which it has for me!), it fosters good discourse and gets to the core of a person's values quickly. Don't be afraid!

9. Conclusion

That's pretty much all the wisdom I have on this subject matter - the rest I'm still learning too! I can tell you that even if you come off reading this on fire and ready to start saving and spending less, it's always easy to fall into bad habits. When I had another jump on the pyramid of massive pay jumps, I fell off my own wagon for a bit and rationalized spending based on percentage of income ("oh, it's only $10").

However, it's pretty easy to hop back on the wagon though once you realize your saving rate isn't where you want it to be. Shame can be a powerful motivator, even if it's self contained.

The bigger picture here is to be open about money and ask others for help/advice. There is a lot of wisdom to be collected if you just put up a social media post that says "trying to open an IRA, anyone have advice?". Google and Reddit can also offer opinions/ideas if you put the energy into trying.

Note: I can't recommend telling everyone your paycheck and how much you have in savings; people will look at you differently, and as mentioned in Chapter 2, they'll expect you to spend a certain way based on your income/savings. However, that is always up to you - focus on **your** goals and what you **need** to achieve them.

And that's the whole point of this book - getting you to where you want to go, one day at a time and one small (instead of large) latte purchase at a time. Good luck!

Appendix: Small "no" Cost Saving Tips

A collection of ideas from Lois and her friends

1. When you go to the grocery store, buy things on sale and craft meals around it

2. Actually, just buy everything that's not a need on sale - challenge yourself to try to do this, especially with clothing. Patience is a virtue!

3. In a pinch, buy frozen veggies instead of fresh… fresh can be healthier for you but frozen is cheaper and doesn't spoil

4. Buy in bulk when you can, especially toilet paper and paper towels. You're always going to need that stuff!

5. Limit yourself to a few movies in the theater a year - just renting and watching at home saves you 75% or so. If you do go, go to a matinee or make it a big treat.

6. Take the time to cook your own meals and freeze ahead of time (frozen burritos!). It will save you a lot of money in the long run.

7. Try to explore public transportation options - bus, bicycle, train, walk, carpool, etc. Driving to work every day is very expensive, and it's not just in gas money. Car maintenance will cost you hundreds every year, and your commuter car will only depreciate in value every year.

8. Keep possessions to a minimum. It is easy to hoard things and see that as "well in case I need this" but it ends up costing you a lot of time and therefore money every time you move or need to clean. Ask yourself if you really need it, and if you don't, then donate it so it goes to someone who does need it. For further reading on this, I recommend Marie Kondo's The Life-Changing Magic of Tidying Up: The Japanese Art of Decluttering and Organizing.

9. Reuse plastic bags - not only better for the environment but saves you from repurchasing little sandwich bags and freezer bags. You can wash them in a dishwasher. I also use tortilla bags, etc. to store things in the freezer.

10. Use fans instead of AC when possible. I understand it may be really hot where you live, but try to mitigate by doing things like closing blinds during the day and opening windows at night when it's cooler. AC is very expensive because it's so energy intensive.

11. Having a lunch box can save you from putting your lunch in some sort of disposable bag every day.

12. Ask yourself can you do it yourself in a reasonable amount of time for less? Like can you replace your floors, fix your bike, etc.? These add up in a big way and you acquire skills. This is an "intangible" aforementioned in Chapter 4.

13. Join a Buy Nothing group on social media. They often have free things available that you may need (i.e. a lamp). It's a great way to both minimize your possessions and find things you need for … free!

14. Order a smaller size when ordering food. This does not apply to clothing!

15. Want to eat out or have a date night? See if there is a Groupon - it's an easy way to save 15% and still have a new/unique experience.

16. Buy flights early. Remember to change your browser or put it on incognito mode because airlines use cookies to track what flights you're looking at and will raise prices on the SEA-DEN flight that you're looking at.

17. Try to opt for easy care professional clothing that doesn't require ironing and professional dry cleaning.

18. When you decide to go clothes shopping and you pick out several items to buy, make yourself put one back.

19. If you're short on time and find yourself eating out often, try to buy frozen pre-prepared meals instead. For less time and slightly less cost, you can get a more nutritious meal.

20. If you live in a cold climate, turn the heat down at home during the day when no one is home. Also, consider investing in warm pjs and, if it's really cold, an electric blanket, instead of heating your whole home.

21. Buy bar shampoo instead of liquid, you usually can get 2-3x the amount of bottled shampoo for the same price.

22. When you do buy clothes, buy nice ones. They'll be better quality and last longer, plus you'll feel "nicer" having nice clothes.

23. Learn to sew to fix said nice clothes when you get a small hole.

24. Avoid subscriptions - even though it's only "$9.99 a month" that means $120 a year. Subscriptions are insidious - they'll keep charging you even if you aren't using the service anymore or you forget. Avoid subscriptions in favor of one off costs.

25. Use a reusable water bottle instead of buying bottled water.

26. Keep showers short, concise, and to the point. You should be able to shower in less than 5 minutes.

27. Space out your haircuts or do them yourself. Long haired individuals probably only need cuts every 6 months.

28. Thrift stores are your friend.

29. Try to live near where you work. Commuting is expensive both in time, energy, and dollars.

30. Need a drink? Try to catch happy hour.

31. Buy a car that you can use for 10+ years, take good care of it, and run it till the bitter end. Or just don't have a car.

32. Don't be afraid to ask for a discount - it's worth a shot, right?

33. Cut coupons and use them, they add up!

34. Slickdeals.net and others have ways that you can set alerts when household items go on sale.

35. Just need a vacation? A lot of airlines have specials where the airfare is significantly reduced for a certain time period if you book ahead. If you don't have a preference and just want to travel, this can be a great way to get instant savings on your exotic vacation.

36. Even if you go to a car shop for repair, buy your own parts first. The markup is quite high when the shop orders and installs (>30%) rather than just install.

37. Try to use a machine washable rag instead of paper towels when possible.

38. Your public library is a great resource for entertainment - you can get books, movies, and lots of media. They also usually have free classes on a weekly basis, which can be a great way to pick up a new skill and meet new people.

39. Learn how to pack your dishwasher efficiently. If you don't have one, wash your dishes together rather than individually to save water.

40. Being sick is expensive, so prioritize your health and take care of yourself. Sleep is cheap but going to the doctor and paying for medicine isn't.

41. Going vegetarian even when just eating out is a great way to save ~20% on meals (i.e. veggie quesadilla versus chicken quesadilla).

42. Setting a hard weekly grocery budget is a good way to make sure you're not overspending on groceries.

43. Some people find itemization of every purchase forces them to look at what and when they are spending. This can push the issue of thoughtful consideration of nonessential (or even essential) items.

44. Turn off lights when you leave the room.

45. Split meals with a friend when you go out to eat.

46. Try to not order a drink with dinner when you go out, especially alcohol. Even if it's only a few dollars, you're effectively adding 20-30% on your meal. Plus, that beer would cost you half as much if you bought it as part of a six pack.

47. Instead of a gym membership, consider joining a group on social media that works out together, whether it's yoga, running, strength training, etc.

48. If you wear makeup, consider what items you really 'need' and get rid of the rest. Makeup goes bad and hoarding it can create this feeling of "needing to have a wide range". The reality is you probably only use a few items regularly and need only a few others for special occasions.

49. Don't buy food on airplanes, bring it with you.

50. With birth control, consider long term options like IUDs. The start up cost can be a lot higher (>$1000) but since they last for years (3-10+) they usually pay for themselves compared to other birth control methods. Use condoms with new partners though - an STD is a lot more expensive than a condom.

References

[1]https://www.tandfonline.com/doi/abs/10.1080/17439760.2014.898316?journalCode=rpos20&

[2]https://www.irs.gov/statistics/soi-tax-stats-individual-statistical-tables-by-size-of-adjusted-gross-income

[3]https://slate.com/business/2016/05/the-latte-is-a-lie-and-buying-coffee-has-nothing-to-do-with-debt-an-excerpt-from-helaine-olens-pound-foolish.html

[4] MacBride, Elizabeth (October 14, 2015). "Jack Bogle: Follow these 4 investing rules—ignore the rest". CNBC.

[5]https://investor.vanguard.com/mutual-funds/profile/VFINX

[6]https://www.acorns.com/earn/foundmoney/

[7]https://www.irs.gov/retirement-plans/plan-participant-employee/retirement-savings-contributions-savers-credit

[8]https://www.rothira.com/roth-ira-limits

[9]https://www.salliemae.com/

[10]https://homeguides.sfgate.com/write-home-mortgage-interest-off-taxes-2019.html

[11]https://www.attomdata.com/news/market-trends/foreclosures/midyear-2018-u-s-foreclosure-market-report/

[12]https://www.valuepenguin.com/average-credit-card-interest-rates

[13]https://www.cardrates.com/advice/credit-card-debt-statistics/

[14] Dew, J. P. (November 2009). Financial issues as predictors of divorce. Paper presented at the annual conference of the National Council on Family Relations. San Francisco, CA